T0105696

'The LORD Said, "*Show My Love!*" So I Will!'

Salvatrice M. Her

WestBow
PRESS
A DIVISION OF THOMAS NELSON

Scripture taken from the Holy Bible, New International Version®. Copyright © 1973, 1978, 1984 Biblica. Used by permission of Zondervan. All rights reserved.

Scripture taken from the New King James Version. Copyright 1979, 1980, 1982 by Thomas Nelson, Inc. Used by permission. All rights reserved.

Scripture taken from Nelson's NKJV Study Bible. Copyright 1997 by Thomas Nelson, Inc. Used by permission. All rights reserved.

WestBow Press books may be ordered through booksellers or by contacting:

WestBow Press
A Division of Thomas Nelson
1663 Liberty Drive
Bloomington, IN 47403
www.westbowpress.com
1-(866) 928-1240

Because of the dynamic nature of the Internet, any web addresses or links contained in this book may have changed since publication and may no longer be valid. The views expressed in this work are solely those of the author and do not necessarily reflect the views of the publisher, and the publisher hereby disclaims any responsibility for them.

Any people depicted in stock imagery provided by Thinkstock are models, and such images are being used for illustrative purposes only.
Certain stock imagery © Thinkstock.

ISBN: 978-1-4497-6232-2 (sc)
ISBN: 978-1-4497-6233-9 (c)
Library of Congress Control Number: 2012914175

Please forward your comments or questions to:
Salvatrice M. Her at: THELORDSAID@hotmail.com

Printed in the United States of America

WestBow Press rev. date: 11/05/2012

HEBREW NAMES OF OUR LORD GOD

Elohim:
Creator
Jehovah:
Covenant Name of God
Adonai:
Master
El Shaddai:
My Supply
My Nourishment
Jehovah-Jireh:
My Provider and My Vision
Jehovah-Rophe:
My Healer
Jehovah-Nissi:
My Victory
Jehovah-M'Kaddesh:
My Sanctifier
Jehovah-Shalom:
My Peace
Jehovah-Tsidkenu:
My Righteousness
Jehovah-Rohi:
My Shepherd
Jehovah-Shammah:
He is there
He is present

MESSAGES FROM THE LORD PRESENTED THROUGH

Salvatrice M. Her

COVER AND ARTWORK

Yvonne Blancaflor Marwede

MANUSCRIPT PREPRATION

Virginia Gabb

'FLOWER' ARTWORK

Salvatrice M. Her

DEDICATION

All the Glory belongs completely to the Father, the Son,
and to the Holy Spirit!
Thank you, sweet LORD Jesus,
for choosing such as me for this task!

Salvatrice

PREFACE

Through the pages of this book, you will find words that speak to your heart and to your spirit!

Many times, our 'mission field', is exactly where we are planted! You can do great things for Him—at this moment!

Before you begin, pray to hear the LORD's voice, as He teaches, encourages, and tells you how much *He Loves You Beyond Measure*!

It is my prayer that you will not hesitate to respond to God Almighty, as Isaiah did:

> *Then I heard the voice of the Lord saying,*
> *"Whom shall I send? And who will go for us?"*
> *And I said, "Here am I. Send me!"*
> ISAIAH 6:8

WHAT OTHERS ARE SAYING ABOUT "THE LORD SAID..." BOOKS

After having read: 'The LORD Said, "Call On Me!" So I Did!' by Salvatrice M. Her, the inspiration and hope these messages convey, would be beneficial if copies could be sent to prisons and hospitals.

Anna M. Ducato

Adult Catechist For Catholic Archdiocese of Los Angeles at St. John Vianney Parish, Hacienda Heights, California

TABLE OF CONTENTS

! GOD'S WITNESS
PROTECTION PROGRAM !

This is the account of Noah. Noah was a righteous man,
blameless among the people of his time, and he walked with
God. Noah had three sons: Shem, Ham and Japheth.
GENESIS 6:9-10

The LORD then said to Noah, "Go into the ark, you and your whole
family, because I have found you righteous in this generation.
GENESIS 7:1

Then they took Jonah and threw him overboard, and the raging sea grew
calm. At this the men greatly feared the LORD, and they offered a sacrifice
to the LORD and made vows to him. But the LORD provided a great fish
to swallow Jonah, and Jonah was inside the fish three days and three nights.
JONAH 1:15-17

O' My Faithful and Obedient Disciple,

How it pleases your LORD GOD...the Almighty One...Who chose the Nation of Israel, through which would be born His Only Begotten Son Who would save His people from their sins!

It pleased the Father of Abraham, Isaac and Jacob, to accept every Gentile, who would believe in JESUS of Nazareth as the risen Messiah... Who Is ALIVE...and speaks through many available scribes in these last days!

Many of you, who are reading or hearing these messages for the first time, have decided to learn more about the CHRIST!

- ♥ Would you truly like to *know* Me?
- ♥ Would you truly like to *spend time* with Me?
- ♥ Would you truly like to *learn* about becoming BORN-AGAIN, and being baptized in the HOLY SPIRIT?
- ♥ Would you truly like to *hear* the Father's Voice...as He speaks within your heart?
- ♥ Would you truly like to *follow* His perfect will for your life, and not what you *think* or *feel* it should or could be?

Many people *think* the Father—Creator and Almighty GOD is He— only listens to prayers of people who think *they, themselves,* are 'holy'!

Many people also *think* that GOD—Merciful and Gracious is He—is too big or too remote to care about the details of their lives!

O precious soul, these are **lies** perpetuated by Satan, himself, who desires for Our Creation to be kept **ignorant** of spiritual truths!

For sin shall not be your master, because you are not under law, but under grace. ROMANS 6:14

† 'Have I not *placed* you under My GRACE?'

† 'Have I not *offered* a Gift so rare…so beyond human comprehension… that it can NOT be bought at any price—save for the Life of My Only Begotten SON?'

† 'Have I not *extended* My complete protection…from Satan…the evil one who would desire to see your precious soul burn in the fires of Hell—reserved for him and his followers?'

Who closed the mouths of the lions…when My servant Daniel was thrown in the den by order of King Darius…for not worshiping, nor praying, to any god—save the One Mighty and True?

Therefore, dearest disciple and friend, have you been too frightened in your *human* state…to trust your GOD…in your *spiritual* state?

"But I am the LORD your God, who brought you out of Egypt. You shall acknowledge no God but me, no Savior except me. HOSEA 13:4

You, cherished friend, reading or hearing this message, at this moment of your life—whether you are a man, woman or child—have been carefully protected and gently guided—ever since the moment you gave your Soul to the Living and True GOD!

† **I AM LORD of lords!** †

† **I AM KING of kings!** †

* I will never leave you, nor ever forsake you, My most treasured **Soul**!

* Your **Spirit** gives Me delight, as it *praises*, *worships*, and *adores* the LORD Almighty!

* When your **Heart** swells with an indescribable and abundant Joy, that renders you speechless, the Angels sing out in Heaven!

* When your **Mind** is always stayed on thoughts of your KING…your *prayers of intercession* are brought before the Father…EL GIBBOR… Mighty is He!

O most blessed friend, your good deeds…done unselfishly and because of your love for Me…bring *joy* to My Heart!

Many circumstances which happen in your life may seem as if your LORD is not aware…and *allows* you to suffer as if I was *punishing* you!

Not so, dear disciple!

+ Have you not experienced *healing* after your brothers and sisters *interceded* on your behalf?
+ Have you not received *forgiveness* from someone you hurt…and swallowed your *pride* to seek sincere forgiveness in all humility?
+ Have I not *closed* and *opened* doors of spiritual and other opportunities, to be for ABBA's Glory?

…Whenever you are down, an angel of the LORD is sent to pick you up!

…Whenever you are tempted by the Enemy to sin against me…I send an angel to show you the way out of that temptation!

At this time, in the history of the world, the Enemy and his cohorts are working feverishly to bring down into his evil and vile encampment the Souls of My faithful and obedient disciples!

You, precious disciple, are who he desires more…**you** and **all** the others who **struggle to resist** the devil!

I, alone, can and will set you free…as you continue to keep your eyes on JESUS, the Messiah—Who speaks to you now!

LISTEN! O man!

HEAR ME! O woman!

† When you are *witnesses* unto Me…I **will** protect you!
† When you *declare* your love for Me… I **will** place My Holy Mantle over you!
† When you *live* each day as a true follower of the Christ…I **will** meet all of your needs according to My *riches in glory*…as you ask the Father in the Name above ALL NAMES—JESUS!

Through the power of the HOLY SPIRIT…**you,** precious believer, are covered by the Blood of the Lamb!

The Scriptures speak for themselves, with the ways the LORD GOD has *protected* Our true friends!

Peter was thrown into prison by order of King Herod and guarded by four squads of four soldiers each! This was sixteen men in all!

So Peter was kept in prison, but the church was earnestly praying to God for him.

The night before Herod was to bring him to trial, Peter was sleeping between two soldiers, bound with two chains, and sentries stood guard at the entrance. Suddenly an angel of the LORD appeared and a light shone in the cell. He struck Peter on the side and woke him up. "Quick, get up!" he said, and the chains fell off Peter's wrists. ACTS 12:5-7

3

After the angel led Peter safely past the guards and out through the iron gate leading to the city...which opened before them...and after walking the length of one street, the angel left him, and Peter came to himself! He was thinking he was part of a vision!

Are you able to even comprehend such a rescue, dear one?

Are you praying for those who are falsely accused and held *because* of their witnessing and professing their faith in the One True SON of GOD—JESUS, the Christ?

There are those of you who are reading or hearing this message...who have experienced this, or are in the midst of it!

Take heart, dearest faithful one!

♥ I AM WITH YOU WHEREVER YOU ARE...
   AND WHEREVER YOU GO...FOR ME!♥

Come! Bow your head for my anointing!

Come! Drink of my Living Water!

Come! Be filled with courage from above!

* Your Savior...JESUS...is coming soon!

* Keep looking up!

I LOVE YOU ABOVE AND BEYOND MEASURE!

Your Blessed Protector,
Yeshua ha'Machiach

! VISIBLE BUT INVISIBLE !

As he neared Damascus on his journey,
suddenly a light from heaven flashed around him.
He fell to the ground and heard a voice say to him,
"Saul, Saul, why do you persecute me?"
"Who are you, Lord?" Saul asked.
"I am Jesus, whom you are persecuting," he replied.
"Now get up and go into the city,
and you will be told what you must do."
The men traveling with Saul stood there speechless;
they heard the sound but did not see anyone.
Saul got up from the ground, but when he opened his eyes he could see nothing.
So they led him by the hand into Damascus. For three days he was blind,
and did not eat or drink anything.
ACTS 9:3-9

O' My Most Dearest Friend,

In accordance with the Father's will, He will take drastic measures to influence one of His children…to accept the FREE GIFT of My SALVATION…through the power of the HOLY SPIRIT!

Paul, whose mission it was to find and kill everyone who followed the CHRIST, was definitely bewildered at being blinded on his way to Damascus!

Instead of living to destroy those who preached the Gospel…he became one of them…and lived only to preach Christ crucified!

His life brought:

♥ **GLORY to the Father!**
  ♥ **PRAISES to the Son!**
    ♥ **THANKSGIVING to the Holy Spirit!**

What of you, dear one?

I addressed you as 'friend', because **you** have made yourself **available** to Glorify the FATHER!

† Do you remember the days in which you, perhaps, *rejected* My invitation?
† Do you remember the days in which you *accepted* My invitation… with unabashed tears of JOY?

✝ Do you remember those days in which you *desired* to shout PRAISES to your KING?

✝ Do you remember in which days *your walk* had become *more difficult?*

✝ Do you remember in which days you became *completely surrendered…* to your LORD?

♥ Those were the days when the Angels in Heaven SHOUTED for JOY!

♥ Those were the days when you brought GLORY TO THE FATHER!

♥ Those were the days when you *sincerely* brought PRAISES TO THE SON!

♥ Those were the days when you *truly* gave THANKSGIVING TO THE HOLY SPIRIT!

? Are you feeling more peace and JOY, My friend?

? Are you feeling more growth in your spiritual walk?

? Are you feeling much closer to your Savior?

Paul *saw* My SHEKINAH GLORY and was blinded for three days! His companions also heard the sound of My voice!

They saw…in Paul…the reaction from his experience!

The visible and the invisible came together in just a few moments!

As it is with any SIN! You do not *see* the SIN! You *see* the *result* of the SIN!

It is only through My Grace that you have been set FREE!

Is not the Father…Who is Mighty…showering all with His unending Mercy?

Did I not come to you…to rescue His Children…His Creation?

Did I not promise to send the Holy Spirit…when I ascended back to Heaven?

Paul wrote to the church in Galatia, as prompted by the HOLY SPIRIT:

So I say, live by the Spirit, and you will not gratify the desires of the sinful nature. For the sinful nature desires what is contrary to the Spirit, and the Spirit what is contrary to the sinful nature. They are in conflict with each other, so that you do not do what you want. But if you are led by the Spirit, you are not under law. GALATIANS 5:16-18

So I, your LORD, ask if you are able to *see* the 'sinful nature' in another… in yourself? NO! However, you can *see the results* of a 'sinful nature'!

…Are there not murders?

…Is there not abandonment?

…Are there not betrayals and rejections?

…Is there not false imprisonment?

…Are there not beatings?

…Is there not apathy and cold-heartedness?

Must I continue?

I, your LORD, know you can think of many more! Especially, if they have infringed upon your own life!

I, your LORD, know you will never find the Father's kind of MERCY from mankind!

You now understand, dearest one?

The *invisible* brings on the hatred and complacency of the *visible*!

My people are expected to shed the 'old man'!

My people are encouraged to put on the New Creation in Christ!

The more you allow Me to fill up your heart, soul, mind and spirit…

…the more we will have an *intimate relationship*!

…the more Glory you will give to our Father, our ABBA…OUR MIGHTY GOD!

…the more sincere thanksgiving you will give to our HOLY SPIRIT!

The more you desire an intimate relationship with your Redeemer…the more you will know what the Father's Perfect Will is for you!

The more you yearn to be **ONE** with ABBA, with the MESSIAH, with the HOLY SPIRIT…the more you will desire to *surrender* your Free Will to your LORD of lords…your KING of kings!

Then, O precious one, you will gain Wisdom, Discernment, Understanding and Truth!

All that I have revealed to you, My chosen friend, is from the FATHER!

"This, then, is how you should pray:
" 'Our Father in heaven,
hallowed be your name,
your kingdom come,
your will be done
on earth as it is in heaven.
Give us today our daily bread.
Forgive us our debts,
as we also have forgiven our debtors.
And lead us not into temptation,
but deliver us from the evil one.'
MATTHEW 6:9-13

When you pray, 'Your Will Be Done', you relinquish your all to ME!

- ♥ Come…dearest cherished one!
- ♥ Come…dearest precious one!
- ♥ Come…dearest chosen one!
- ♥ Come…dearest loved one!

Jesus answered, "I am the way and the truth and the life. No one comes to the Father except through me. If you really knew me, you would know My Father as well. From now on, you do know him and have seen him." JOHN 14:6-7

What is now **invisible** to you…will become **visible**…when I return for you!

I LOVE YOU BEYOND TIME ETERNAL!

Your Intimate Friend,
   Jesus

! I WILL MEET YOU ANYWHERE !

So do not fear, for I am with you; do not be dismayed,
for I am your God. I will strengthen you and help you; I
will uphold you with my righteous right hand.
ISAIAH 41:10

O' My Dearest Disciple,

STOP and LOOK! Where are you at this very moment…as you read or hear these words?

They have been written just for you! Just for now! Difficult to believe?

Did I not promise to be with you…always? This means that I, the Christ, JEHOVAH-shammah, am with you at any moment of any day… and wherever you happen to be!

† Are you in a place that you would not mind, if I, the LORD, would accompany you?
† You could be in a church, synagogue, market, hospital, prison, brothel, tavern, school, home…or anywhere else!
† Does it *matter* where you are, dear one?
† You may think you are in a place that I, the LORD, would never enter! However, because of My love for you, I will be where you are!
† You could *think* of Me…anywhere!
† You could *reach out* for Me…anywhere…and at any time!

I addressed you as, 'Dearest Disciple'! Do you wonder why? It is because **YOU** have been searching for **ME**…throughout your life! You have been drawn close to **ME**…many times! Then, because of people or circumstances in your life, you turned away!

Remember what I said through Isaiah, and then through My servant Paul…who continued to teach, though he was living under guard in Rome!

There were many disagreements, as he told them about My Grace, and that I am the promised Messiah…as taught by the Law of Moses, and then through the prophets!

I was standing next to Paul as they disagreed among themselves, and began to leave, after Paul had made this final statement:

…*"The Holy Spirit spoke the truth to your forefathers when he said through Isaiah the prophet:*

" 'Go to this people and say, "You will be ever hearing but never understanding; you will be ever seeing but never perceiving." For this people's heart has become calloused; they hardly hear with their ears, and they have closed their eyes. Otherwise they might see with their eyes, hear with their ears, understand with their hearts and turn, and I would heal them.'

"Therefore I want you to know that God's salvation has been sent to the Gentiles, and they will listen!" ACTS 28:25-28

Are you a Gentile…blessed disciple?

Or are you a Jew, just as I was? Does this surprise you?

Have you not spoken to some who would argue the fact of the Christ's blood-line? This truth bothers many…so they choose to ignore it! However, it does not change the truth!

What is most *important* for you…about ME?

Is it My Love?

Is it My Grace?

Is it My Power?

Is it My Promises?

Is it My Unconditional Love?

Is it My Forgiveness of your sins?

What is most *important* for ME…about YOU?

♥ It is your *willingness to love Me*, your LORD of lords…above and beyond any one or any thing else in your life…

…with all your soul!

…with all your mind!

…with all your heart!

…with all your spirit!

Remember, dear one, to love others *above* and *beyond* yourself!

I have told you this so that my joy may be in you and that your joy may be complete. My command is this: Love each other as I have loved you. Greater love has no one than this, that he lay down his life for his friends. You are my friends if you do what I command. JOHN 15:11-14

Remember: I Am Omni-present!

KNOW THIS: I AM NEAR YOU…**night and day**!

What will **you** do when situations begin to seem out of control?

† Will you continue to know that **I am near you**?

† Will you continue to cling only to ME!

Being **in** the world, means that you are human, born of a woman! However, YOU ARE NOT OF THIS WORLD!

† You **belong** where I AM!

You will have nothing to fear when you hear the Trumpet blast, and your name is called out…and you will be changed in the *blink of an eye*!

You will meet ME in the air…because YOU ANSWERED MY CALL TO BECOME **BORN AGAIN**!

Remember: the Holy Spirit will teach you and give you Wisdom, Discernment, Knowledge, Understanding, and Spiritual Insight!

O My dearest disciple! It is a JOY to teach you!

But seek first his kingdom and his righteousness, and all these things will be given to you as well. MATTHEW 6:33

Come…to the Throne Room!

Come…spend time with Me upon awakening each day!

Come…call upon My Name and partake of My Living Water!

Will you not take hold of My hand?

I LOVE YOU BEYOND MEASURE
AND I HAVE CHOSEN YOU
TO CONTINUE MY WORK ON EARTH!

I AM WHO AM,
    Yeshua ha'Machiach,
    Jesus the Messiah

! DO YOU EVER WONDER? !

Cast your bread upon the waters,
For you will find it after many days.
Give a serving to seven, and also to eight,
For you do not know what evil will be on the earth.
ECCLESIASTES 11:1-2 NKJV

As you do not know what is the way of the wind,
Or how the bones grow in the womb
of her who is with child,
So you do not know the works
of God who makes everything.
ECCLESIASTES 11:5 NKJV

Consider the work of God;
For who can make straight what He has made crooked?
In the day of prosperity be joyful,
But in the day of adversity consider:
Surely God has appointed the one as well as the other,
So that man can find out nothing that will come after him.
ECCLESIASTES 7:13-14 NKJV

O' My Dear and Blessed Disciple,

The Father…our ABBA…desires for ME to answer questions you have…and have always wondered about!

Have you wondered at Solomon's words:

'Cast your bread upon the waters'?…'You will find it after many days'?

Do you not need bread and water to sustain life?

Are you unselfish enough to share what you have to eat and to drink? *It will return*! You will not lack…because what you share will be returned to you sevenfold or tenfold from Me…or through those whom I will choose!

Have you wondered at My Words:

My command is this: Love each other as I have loved you. Greater love has no one than this, that he lay down his life for his friends. You are my friends if you do what I command. JOHN 15:12-14

♥ Loving ME, your LORD, more than *the comfort of your friends*!

- ♥ Loving ME, your LORD, more than *their problems*! More than *their wants or desires*!
- ♥ Should you not allow ME, the LORD of lords, to work in their lives?
- ♥ Do you not trust ME, the KING of kings?

Being overly concerned, and using one of the worst human emotions…WORRY…throws you *directly* into Satan's nets!

Do you understand what I am telling you, dear one? This eye-opener can be overwhelming!

I did not die to supply Our creation with worldly comforts! Riches! Property! Fame! Happiness on Earth! Freedom from war or adversity!

Think, dear one!

Not one of these is available on Earth for *free*!

You were created to live in a Paradise! However, you **can** receive all and more! Spiritual Treasures unsurpassed! It is quite *simple*! You can give away **one** thing, and receive it all…**on this Earth**!

'What is it' you ask?

- † The *purchase price* is: GIVING YOUR IMMORTAL SOUL TO SATAN!!!
- † **I DIED to SAVE your SOUL from Satan!**
- † **I ROSE for you to know that WITH ME you will have ETERNAL LIFE in the NEW HEAVEN and on the NEW EARTH!**
- † However, you must *know how to live,* so that you will *know how to die*!
- † **You must know what will happen to you *after* you die!**

YOU MUST CHOOSE!

Tell others: No one can choose this for you…as if it were a gift purchased from a marketplace! I Am the only One Who can GIVE you this Gift! And it is NOT a TEMPORARY GIFT…like flowers, which die after plucked from their roots!

Think, dear one!

You must understand all of this, even into the very depths of your soul! This is the **only way** you can set yourself apart from those you love, and allow ME to work in their lives!

Allow ME…with the Power of the Holy Spirit…to reach the depths of *their* souls!

Will you *allow* ME to *speak and act* through you when the *time is right*? To do so…otherwise…may cause a soul to be lost…forever!

Your assignment…*first and foremost*…is to give PRAISE and GLORY to the FATHER! Then…when you are *desirous* to do this…and **only** this…

will you be ready to be given an Assignment for the KINGDOM…by EL GIBBOR…Most High GOD ALMIGHTY!

You will then be aware of the *promptings* and the *voice* of the Holy Spirit!

I will give you every place where you set your foot, as I promised Moses. JOSHUA 1:3

Will you live to be *blameless*?

When Abram was ninety-nine years old, the LORD appeared to him and said, "I am God Almighty; walk before me and be blameless. I will confirm my covenant between me and you and will greatly increase your numbers." GENESIS 17:1-2

Could you, dear one, or would you, faithful disciple, walk *blameless* before ME?

Are you wondering all you have been reading or hearing?

- ♥ Do you wonder why I call 'adversity' a blessing?
- ♥ Do you wonder why I say, *'Greater love has no one than to lay down his life for his friends'*?

You do not need to *wonder*!

Did I not say, in the hearing of My first disciples:

I no longer call you servants, because a servant does not know his master's business. Instead, I have called you friends, for everything that I learned from my Father I have made known to you. JOHN 15:15

Therefore, wonder no more! You will know *and* understand all Earthly and Heavenly mysteries…at the perfect time chosen by the Father!

Therefore, work diligently at all I have chosen you to do!

DO NOT ALLOW anything nor anyone, to come between you and your LORD, the CHRIST!

WATCH! LOOK UP! LISTEN!

Come! Allow Me to anoint you *daily*!

Come! Use My anointing *wisely*!

Come! Drink of My *Living* Water!

Come! Eat of My *Blessed* Bread!

O dear faithful and obedient disciple, My beloved friend!

…**Seek wisdom**! Not for personal gain…but for Heaven's!

…**Seek righteousness**! Not for personal blessing…but for God!

I LOVE YOU…BEYOND MEASURE!

Your Master and Friend,
   Jesus

Precious Sweet-one:

The world and its desires pass away,
but the man who does the will of God lives forever.
1 JOHN 2:17

HEAVENLY TREASURES LAST...
EARTHLY PLEASURES ARE SOON PAST!
CHRIST-QUOTE by SMH

! WHEN IS MY *TIMING* PERFECT !

"No one knows about that day or hour, not even the angels in heaven, nor the Son, but only the Father. As it was in the days of Noah, so it will be at the coming of the Son of Man.
MATTHEW 24:36-37

But I trust in you, O LORD; I say, "You are my God." My times are in your hands; deliver me from my enemies and from those who pursue me. Let your face shine on your servant; save me in your unfailing love.
PSALM 31:14-16

A friend loves at all times,…
PROVERBS 17:17

O' My Dear and Faithful Friend,

There is much PURE LOVE waiting for all My friends, in our Eternal World!

You are unable to *comprehend* what I tell you, now! However, as you draw *closer and closer* to ME…your BLESSED LORD…your *human mind* will begin to grasp much spiritual knowledge!

As you gain this spiritual knowledge, you will also learn to understand what I need you to do for the Kingdom! This *understanding* will then give *light* to spiritual discernment! This is for your *soul's protection*!

Remember…your Enemy, and Mine, prowls the earth looking for someone to devour! He uses many *tricks*…at a *perfect time*…through the *perfect person*…or *perfect situation*! Be alert, dear one! Use your knowledge of discernment…*wisely*!

This is why I gave you the Holy Spirit…when I left Earth as the Son of Man, and went to be with My Father in Heaven!

As I live…so will **you** LIVE with Me, precious friend!

I must tell you, when you SEEK ME…when you OBEY ME…when you SEARCH FOR ME…when you HONOR ME above all others…you are *glorifying* our ABBA!

Through all this, the Holy Spirit fills you with more JOY, more PEACE, more LOVE…Blessed Gifts from our ABBA! Does this surprise you?

These things are all in My Living Waters! The more you drink, the more you will receive from the Father! Our MIGHTY GOD…EL-GIBBOR!

Come…desiring for more! There is much work to be done before My return!

Meanwhile, live for that day! Watch for the spiritual and worldly *traps*, which the Enemy sets…in places that can surely fool you!

Pray as David did:

My salvation and my honor depend on God; he is my mighty rock, my refuge. Trust in him at all times, O people; pour out your hearts to him, for God is our refuge. Selah PSALM 62:7-8

When will *you* be ready to take refuge in ME?

† Am I NOT the LORD of lords?

† Am I NOT the KING of kings?

♥ Do I not know your heart?

♥ Do I not understand your spirit?

♥ Do I not have *your name* written in the Lamb's Book of Life?

♥ Do I not send My Warrior Angels to protect your very SOUL?

♥ Do I not pray to the Father for your MIND to choose correctly?

† There is never a time when you are being tempted…that I do not show you a way out!

† There is never a time when you are weak…that I will not strengthen you!

† There is never a time when you are crying out in grief…that I will not comfort you!

There have been many times, when I, the LORD, have waited for you to cry out for ME! During these times, you tried to do things in *your own strength*!

Are these not the times you came to ME…in remorse…crying for forgiveness?

† There is **never** a time that is right for you to *ignore* ME!

† There is **never** a time to think I am too *busy* to look upon you!

† There is **never** a time to doubt My *loving sacrifice* for you!

…The time is *always perfect* to let go of the world around you!

…The time is *always perfect* to spend part of your day *listening* to My Voice!

…The time is *always perfect* to tell others of *your* love for Me!

In these days, too many people…including family and friends…are pulling at you from every direction! If those who are *grabbing* at you, do NOT know your LORD…they will grab at you more!

WHY? To see how much you *truly* LOVE ME! How *truly* you *believe* all that **YOU** tell them about **ME**!

There are many choices you must make…every day! The Enemy sneaks into these choices! He tells you, that if you go out with these *unsaved* friends, you will have an *opportunity* to 'save them'! You decide this is a 'good idea', and you go out with them! However, they persuade you 'to take just one little drink…it won't hurt…and you will show you are one of them'…then you forget all about ME!

You see, dearest one, you have no need to go into the devil's playpen to tell others about Me! As you honor your walk with Me…the Holy Spirit will place you in the perfect situations…in My perfect timing!

The Holy Spirit will also tell you what to say…at the perfect time!

Following the Enemy's temptations…to **think** you will win one soul…is like stepping into a ring of fire…trying to douse it with one cup of water!

However, by staying out of that ring of fire, you will be able to put it out…with My Living Waters…*when hearts are ready*…and at the perfect time…is when *souls* are *won*!

Come! Stand in My Shadow…as I will protect you!

Come! Wait for Me…to guide you!

**I LOVE YOU, DEAREST FRIEND,
BEYOND MEASURE!**

Your Redeemer,
  Jesus

Precious **S**weet-one:

> *…As I was with Moses, so I will be with you;
> I will never leave you nor forsake you.*
> JOSHUA 1:5

! WHERE IS YOUR HEART? !

Create in me a clean heart, O God,
And renew a steadfast spirit within me.
Do not cast me away from Your presence,
And do not take Your Holy Spirit from me.
Restore to me the joy of Your salvation,
And uphold me by Your generous Spirit.
PSALM 51:10-12 NKJV

O' My Faithful Disciple,

The Father, your ABBA, knows...and has known...your *heart*!

Your *heart* is the *physical life* within you...since the moment you were born!

The *heart* He gave you was pure! A purity that can not be even imagined by the human mind!

- ♥ This purity is *born* in Heaven!
- ♥ This purity was *ordained* before the beginning of time!
- ♥ This purity is *seen* in the *eyes* of a new-born baby!
- ♥ This purity is *seen and felt* in the arms of a small and very young child!
- ♥ This purity is *shining through* the innocence of a disabled child, who cannot even speak...nor hear!

Have you not seen one of these...of My most precious creations?

If you ever have the opportunity to meet even one, you will *feel a bit of Heaven*...and My Presence!

Remember...and tell others...these children who were born...less than what the world thinks is perfect...are actually My special Angels...sent to Earth to test the hearts of humans!

Uniting these precious Angels with the 'perfect' parents, is a miracle only your LORD GOD could accomplish!

- † What have you said or thought, when you have seen a 'deformed' baby?
- † What have family or friends said or thought, when they have encountered a child born blind?
- † Or...a child missing a limb...or maybe two?
- † Or...a child whose brain has been damaged in childbirth?

Where are the hearts...the **true hearts**...at these times?

Would your heart accept one of these precious Angels?

Do not answer just to 'please' Me...your LORD of lords! Remember, I see and know your innermost heart! I have, from the moment you were born! It was I, the LORD, Who brought you out of the womb! You trusted Me even at your mother's breast!

From birth...you were cast upon Me!

From your mother's womb...I have been your GOD!

David, a man after My own heart, wrote Psalms which were sung to Me! He did not just *utter words*! He *uttered* them with music, which *flowed* from his heart!

What of you, dearest one?

Have you heard of My Prophet Joel? He lived during the *terrible* days, when the Babylonian army destroyed Jerusalem! He saw leading citizens of Judah...who survived...carried into captivity to Babylon! These were the very ones, which Joel was trying to warn!

He cited the attacks of the locusts as an example how the Father, God Almighty, would use a natural disaster to try and awaken the people to repentance!

"Now, therefore," says the LORD,
"Turn to Me with all your heart,
With fasting, with weeping, and with mourning."
So rend your heart, and not your garments;
Return to the LORD your God,
For He is gracious and merciful,
Slow to anger, and of great kindness;
And He relents from doing harm. JOEL 2:12-13 NKJV

However, even to this day, many of My chosen people, Israel, still 'harden their hearts'! They 'turn deaf ears' to *My Pleadings*! Joel told them what the Holy Spirit was telling him!

One day...they will fall on their faces...*seeking*...even *pleading* for forgiveness!

What of you, My dear one? You still allow the world to pull you far from your LORD! Why?

Does your heart not belong to Me—

from *EVERLASTING to EVERLASTING?*

DO YOU BELONG TO ME?

As I am the LORD of your heart, why do you *crowd* Me out with pieces of the world?

…Pieces of the world—crying or complaining about what you do not have! What may not be necessary!

…Pieces of the world—falling into self-pity!

…Pieces of the world—allowing those in your life to *steal* your JOY, your PEACE, your TIME with ME!

…Pieces of the world—trying to please *MEN*…rather than ME…the Savior of your soul!

…Pieces of your heart given to the world—**should include**: doing your part in helping to feed the poor, visit the sick, and those in prison! Also, to be mindful of the needs of widows and orphans!

These acts of love, and true compassion, are filling up your Heavenly Home, and causing a child, or a stranger to turn to Me!

Come! Let ME, your LORD, help you *place your heart* in My hand!

Come! Let Me, your KING, do all the *heart* stretching!

Come! Let the HOLY SPIRIT fill your heart, which *feeds* the brain, which gives *words* to the tongue to bless or…? What do you think? What will you do?

✝ I AM WHO AM…
LOVES YOU BEYOND THE WORLD!
✝ DO NOT ALLOW YOUR SOUL'S HEART TO
FALL INTO THE WRONG HANDS! IT IS THE
MOST PRECIOUS TREASURE YOU OWN!

Your Faithful Lover,
   Jesus

Precious Sweet-one:

Let the words of my mouth and the meditation of my heart
Be acceptable in Your sight,
O LORD, my strength and my Redeemer.
PSALM 19:14 NKJV

CHRIST-QUOTE:
SERVING LOTS OF LOVE…
IS NOT FATTENING!
SMH

! WHY DO YOU DO THAT? !

"Therefore I tell you, do not worry about your life, what you will eat or drink; or about your body, what you will wear. Is not life more important than food, and the body more important than clothes? Look at the birds of the air; they do not sow or reap or store away in barns, and yet your heavenly Father feeds them. Are you not much more valuable than they? Who of you by worrying can add a single hour to his life?
MATTHEW 6:25-27

O' My Dear and Obedient Follower of the KING,

Today, like many other days, you have called upon Me to give you Wisdom, Guidance, Understanding and Discernment! Have you not? Then…you go about the busyness of your day! Our ABBA watches…as He stands on the balcony to the Throne Room!

Your GOD watches to see when you will speak to Him—with thanks and praise—for answering your prayers!

He knows that *He will supply* all you need for today!

Do **you** believe that He will keep this promise?

And my God will meet all your needs according to his glorious riches in Christ Jesus. PHILIPPIANS 4:19

Therefore, I, the LORD of lords, ask you: 'Why have you been purchasing and hoarding so many *things*? Do you not trust ABBA's promises?

Think, dear follower! Think back over your life!

Has He **ever broken** a promise?

This should be easy to remember, because it would be a momentous occasion! Would it not?

You are not alone in attempting to store food and supplies for a 'rainy day'! After all, do not the squirrels do this, to last throughout the winter months?

Has not the God of the Universe…The Creator…placed this survival instinct in animals such as these? Yes…and it has been placed in humans as well!

* However, humans are said to have 'common sense'!
* Humans are to *understand* they have a Supreme Creator!

My dearest disciple, **you**, **alone**, were created in Our Image! The Image of the FATHER, and the SON, and the HOLY SPIRIT!

✝ The Son of Man did NOT die on the Cross for the animals, which were placed on the Earth to be subservient to man!

✝ The SON of MAN is the **SON OF GOD...THE LIVING GOD!**

Do I not love you **more** than the birds in the air, and the animals on the Earth, and the fish in the sea?

"And why do you worry about clothes? See how the lilies of the field grow. They do not labor or spin. Yet I tell you that not even Solomon in all his splendor was dressed like one of these. If that is how God clothes the grass of the field, which is here today and tomorrow is thrown into the fire, will he not much more clothe you, O you of little faith? MATTHEW 6:28-30

Is this not a puzzlement to you in these modern times?

I tell you, My dearest one, men and women have been the same since the days of Adam and Eve, when their first *clothing* was made of leaves!

They covered their bodies—because they recognized the fact they had sinned—against Almighty GOD!

They sinned by disobeying their Creator!

...Are you not doing the same?

...Are you not covering your body with the best and finest materials you can buy?

...Are you not looking for clothing, which will impress others?

Why? Is not the purpose of clothing to cover up your bodies against earthly elements?

If you know that your LORD is Omnipresent—EVERYWHERE— then how can you ignore that fact?

Is this what you teach your children? That 'sin' is okay, since I can not be seen with the human eye? Why?

You **know**...do you NOT? It is because **you** do not *understand how and why you, and no one else, can neither see, nor hear your LORD!*

One day soon, **YOU WILL HEAR ME! YOU WILL SEE ME!** Then it will be **JUDGMENT TIME!**

However, those of you I love dearly...I rebuke and I discipline!

Do you not rebuke your children, or discipline them, always being gentle, yet firm?

Be perfect, therefore, as your heavenly Father is perfect. MATTHEW 5:48

You know what sins you have committed, and continue to commit! You know **why** you have committed these particular sins...do you NOT?

Each time the temptation comes…you must chase the Enemy from entering the *door of your heart!*

In many Messages, I, your LORD, have told you of a simple, but powerful prayer, for any temptation:

Call to Me: *'JESUS! The Enemy is knocking at the door of my heart! Please answer it! Thank you! AMEN!'*

Then…take your mind quickly from the situation!

Worrying…will only invite the Enemy into your territory! So do *not worry*, My blessed follower!

But seek first his kingdom and his righteousness, and all these things will be given to you as well. Therefore do not worry about tomorrow, for tomorrow will worry about itself. Each day has enough trouble of its own. MATTHEW 6:33-34

Do not allow the *spirit of worry*…to use even a drop of your precious spiritual strength!

…Use your strength…spiritual, mental, emotional, physical and financial…to bring **GLORY TO THE FATHER!**

…Use your spiritual strength to show others *unconditional love!*

…Use your spiritual strength to fill every fiber of your being with *peace!*

…Use your spiritual strength to *glow with My JOY* for…

DIVINE ENCOUNTERS!
DIVINE DELAYS!
DIVINE ASSIGNMENTS!

♥ Seek the Holy Spirit to orchestrate your days!

♥ Come! Do not do that which will pull you away from ME!

I WILL ALWAYS LOVE YOU…
BEYOND MEASURE1

I AM BLESSED TO LEAD…WHEN YOU DESIRE TO FOLLOW!

The Christ,
Jesus

! DO THEY COME WHEN YOU INVITE THEM? !

Sow for yourselves righteousness, reap the fruit of unfailing love,
and break up your unplowed ground; for it is time to seek the
LORD, until he comes and showers righteousness on you.
HOSEA 10:12

O' My Dearest Disciples,

Our *ABBA* loves you more than you know! You may *say* that you know…because He sent His only Son!

However, if you have had understanding beyond that, this is because you are His Creation! I am sure that you love anything which you have created…do you not? Are not your children, whom you helped create, your treasures?

I call you to gather with Me! I call many; however, only a few answer!

How many were healed by My hand when I walked on Earth? The number is unknown…except to the Father!

How many returned to thank Me? Not many! This surprises you?

How many returned to…

…Listen to Me teach?

…To pray with Me?

…To help me?

…To feed Me?

…To give Me fresh clothing?

…To give Me a bed to sleep in?

You, today, would think there had to be many! "After all," you say, "You fed the 5,000, LORD!"

How many were there the day so many cried out for Me to be *crucified?* The sadness of the numbers would overwhelm you!

✝ Yes, I was *crucified*! I died on the Cross!

✝ My heart was broken a long time before that, over those who were ungrateful! Have you been *ungrateful?*

✝ Do you feel sad when those whom you have invited to pray with you…do not come? When you invite those who do come…and they come, perhaps once…or even twice…and then they come no longer…do you not wonder?

…Do you think *you* are doing something wrong?

...Do you think *you* could do something better to give them a desire to come and gather?

♥ To LEARN of Me?
♥ To PRAISE Me?

It is the same today as it was when I was on Earth! They thought *I* was strange! Many came because they were curious!

However, I touched a part of them...**so deep**...they had to *run from* Me!

Those of you who are doing My will, and calling others to gather to Honor Me, to Love Me, to ADORE Me, to WORSHIP and PRAISE Me, do not understand, that many do not desire to go that **spiritually deep**!

Your desire to have others experience what you have and still do...is a blessing to the FATHER...to the SON...to the HOLY SPIRIT!

Do NOT be concerned! **I must** 'speak' with them in another way!

I CALL MANY! I CHOOSE A FEW!

Those of you who continue to be faithful, are to continue to grow in your relationship with Me!

♥ PRAY for them, My disciples!
♥ PRAY for them, My cherished ones!
♥ PRAY for them, that their *ears* will finally be opened!
♥ PRAY for them, so that they will *see* and their *hearts* will be ready, and they will run to gather with those who love Me!

But you must have Holy Indifference when you pray! You cannot allow for *disappointments*! Remember? Have I not told you this, many times?

There is something, dear ones, you will not like to hear! One day, when those who were invited, and did not come...they will *desire* to gather with you! However, *you* will not be available! You will not be on the Earth any longer! They will search! They will cry! The anguish they will feel...if they did not come at the first or the second, even the third invitation...will be more than their *hearts can bear*!

Do not be concerned...those are for Me...**I will reach them**...if their hearts are sincere and true!

♥ Continue to gather, My cherished ones, with those who **truly** desire to PRAISE ME!
♥ Those who **truly** desire to FEEL MY TOUCH!
♥ Those who **truly** desire to FEEL MY PRESENCE!

They will come, but they will come with TRUE HEARTS...to give and not to take! Do you understand, dear ones?

Many *know* what you are doing! Many *know* what you are all about! But they are *fearful* of you, because they can *feel* the Holy Spirit around you!

† You **pray,** and you **speak,** and you **glow** with authority!
† You go **through** pain, and all other terrible situations, which would normally bring despair…but you are *not* despaired!
† You are *not* in the pit!
† You are *not* sad!
† You show *no* self-pity!

They cannot understand this! They think there is something wrong with you!

Did not the people…even My friends and family… think there was something wrong with ME?

Continue to be joyful, My dear ones, because you are in My circle…do you not feel *peace* and *joy*, that I am in *yours?*

It is the *Enemy* who tries to keep them away! The Father allows it…to see how they *truly love Me!* To see if they will not allow anything to hinder them!

When you gather…I will be there! Make a joyful noise! Dance and sing!

My angels will join you! Do not doubt! My angels look forward to whenever My true chosen gather to bring GLORY, HONOR, and ADORATION to:

♥ The FATHER!
  ♥ The SON!
    ♥ The HOLY SPIRIT!

Come! You Are Loved Beyond Any Measure…and it is the measure of Heaven that I speak of…not the way the world measures!!

I Am your Lover and Friend!

I Am the One Who has called you!

I Am the One Who has made you Mine!

I AM,
  Jesus

! WHO IS IN THE MIRROR? !

"For God did not send His Son into the world to
condemn the world, but that the world
through him might be saved.
"He who believes in Him is not condemned,
but he who does not believe is condemned already, because he has
not believed in the name of the only begotten Son of God.
"And this is the condemnation, that the light has come into the world, and
men loved darkness rather than light, because their deeds were evil.
JOHN 3:17-19 NKJV

O' My Most Beloved Disciple,

Listen to your LORD GOD with the inner-most parts of your *heart*, your *mind*, your *soul*, and your *spirit*!

Even your physical ears shall hear Me...though you may be deaf... because My Voice is heard from within for now...and one day you will be completely in the Presence of the LORD KING...and we will speak face-to-face!

Just as I spoke with many of Our disciples, in days of old, I, the LORD of lords, speak to you now...in these last days!

Therefore, cherished disciple, **fear not** of all you see and hear in today's world!

The evil that surrounds My chosen people, will not exist for much longer!

This is the reason I am speaking through many messengers, many scribes, around the Earth!

Those of Our dearest disciples, who make themselves available...at any hour of day or night...are precious in the sight of EL GIBBOR—GOD ALMIGHTY!

These disciples serve others in a myriad of ways...
faithfully and *obediently*...with complete unselfishness
...and loving dedication!

All those who serve family or friends—are serving **Me**—JESUS, the Messiah!

Did I not come into the world to *serve* and *save* the lost sheep of Israel? **YES!**

Did I not offer this same Saving Mercy and Grace to all Gentiles, who would believe and give themselves completely to Me? Yes…for this pleased and blessed the Father—EL GIBBOR—GOD ALMIGHTY!

Therefore, have you, dear disciple, who is ever discerning of writings through other messengers, looked in the mirror to be sure your attire is pleasing to others you may meet?

What about *Me?*

How do *you* look to GOD?

Where do *you see* the LORD?

For you were once darkness, but now you are light in the Lord. Walk as children of light (for the fruit of the Spirit is in all goodness, righteousness, and truth), finding out what is acceptable to the Lord. EPHESIANS 5:8-10 NKJV

Have you seen My Light in the eyes of others?

Be assured—these are My *truest* disciples!

What of your eyes, dear one?

Is there *light*—My Light—shining through as love…as forgiveness…as unconditional acceptance of others…for the LORD of lords?

- ♥ Look into a mirror as you *praise* Me!
- ♥ Look into a mirror as you *pray* for the needs of family and friends!
- ♥ Look into a mirror as you *seek* forgiveness of your sins!
- ♥ Look into a mirror as you *ask* to have favor of GOD in all circumstances!
- ♥ Look into a mirror and *offer* a **sacrifice of praise and adoration** for tears of grief and in **all** painful situations!

Is this difficult to accomplish, dear one?

- † Did I not thank the Father for His *good* and *perfect will* to sacrifice His only begotten Son…to redeem mankind from the clutches of Satan?
- † Did I not die a physical death…with My Blood, shed as the ultimate sacrifice…the most Perfect Lamb of the Living GOD?
- † Did I not raise from the grave and **conquer** the spirit of Death… once and for all?

Then, blessed disciple, sing praises with words of adoration, and rejoice *in* and *for* My agony on the Cross…for all the *pain* and *suffering* which the Father is allowing in your life!

Look in the mirror…what do you see?

- ✦ Is your face serene?
- ✦ Is your face filled with stress?
- ✦ Is your face showing delight?

Look in the mirror...who do you see?

- Is your face resembling a loving person...or a hateful one?
- Is your face resembling one overtaken by grief...or gladness?
- Is your face resembling one from a heavenly dimension...or overtaken by the evils of the world?

Whoever believes that Jesus is the Christ is born of God, and everyone who loves Him who begot also loves him who is begotten of Him.

By this we know that we love the children of God, when we love God and keep His commandments.

For this is the love of God, that we keep His commandments. And His commandments are not burdensome.

For whatever is born of God overcomes the world. And this is the victory that has overcome the world—our faith.

Who is he who overcomes the world, but he who believes that Jesus is the Son of God? 1 JOHN 5:1-5 NKJV

Is the LORD of lords not GOD's Witness?

GOD...EL GIBBOR...the Almighty...LIVING and TRUE... ELOHIM...CREATOR OF ALL...the HEAVENS...the EARTH... ABOVE AND BENEATH!

This is He who came by water and blood—Jesus Christ; not only by water, but by water and blood. And it is the Spirit who bears witness, because the Spirit is truth.

For there are three that bear witness in heaven: the Father, the Word, and the Holy Spirit; and these three are one. 1 JOHN 5:6-7 NKJV

You, beloved one, who is reading or hearing these messages have been blessed by the Father!

...You have been chosen by the SON!

...You have received into your *heart*...into your *mind*...into your *spirit*... the HOLY SPIRIT!

Through the same HOLY SPIRIT you can communicate with the FATHER through JESUS, the MESSIAH!

- ♥ You, beloved friend, have been filled with the peace that surpasses human understanding!
- ♥ You, cherished one, have accepted the Anointed Gift of Salvation freely...and offered back to GOD...your Free Will!
- ♥ You, blessed heart, have chosen joy over sadness

...which pleases the LORD GOD!

Look into the mirror!

…Tell Me…**what** do you see now, after reading or hearing these words, through the power of the Holy Spirit?

…Tell Me…**Who** do you see now, after filling your mind's heart with this message?

Look and **see** the JOY of the LORD and KING!

Look and **see** Christ JESUS shining on your face and His smile on your lips!

Look and **see** your Salvation sparkling from your eyes!

Is not the JOY of your LORD that which gives strength in all circumstances?

Look into the mirror…not for worldly vanity, nor for human pride… but to see your *spiritual light!*

"Let your light so shine before men, that they may see your good works and glorify your Father in heaven. MATTHEW 5:16 NKJV

Seek discernment and spiritual insight from the Holy Spirit…and understand the words from your LORD!

Ask for My Joy to fill your heart and mind and spirit!

Then…My dear and beloved disciple…look into the mirror…tell Me now—Who do you see looking at you!

Is it not My Image?

If so…then others will also see your LORD!

Be aware, dear one, many will rebuff you if they sense My Light and My Holy Spirit surrounding you!

This is great reason to rejoice!

Come…Rejoice in the Presence of the LORD!

Come…Worship and Adore the KING of kings!

Come…Praise your Father Who created you!

I AM HE WHO LOVES YOU

BEYOND MEASURE!

Look in the Mirror and See the Joy of thy Salvation!

Forever Your Savior,
   Yeshua ha'Machiach

! TAKE ADVANTAGE OF SERVING !

And if it seems evil unto you to serve the LORD, choose you this day
whom you will serve; whether the gods which your fathers served that
were on the other side of the flood, or the gods of the Amorites, in whose
land ye dwell: but as for me and my house, we will serve the LORD.
JOSHUA 24:15 NKJV

Jesus said to him, "Away from me, Satan! For it is written:
'Worship the Lord your God, and serve him only.' "
Then the devil left him, and angels came and attended him.
MATTHEW 4:10-11

O' My Most Obedient Disciple,

Are **you**, dear one, truly obedient?

Why did I choose Jonah to go to Nineveh?

Did your LORD decide to punish Jonah for his decision to run from Me?

Jonah *knew* that the LORD **would** punish him for **trying to run** from the **ALL-SEEING EYE OF GOD!**

Most people only remember that Jonah was in the belly of the whale for three days! Then:

From inside the fish Jonah prayed to the LORD his God. He said: "In my distress I called to the LORD and he answered me. From the depths of the grave I called for help, and you listened to my cry. JONAH 2:1-2

Jonah prayed…seeking *forgiveness* for TRYING to hide from the LORD GOD, because Jonah's fear was in going to Nineveh!

On the ship to Tarshish, he witnessed to the sailors…and *admitted* his sin of *running* from **his** God!

After the sailors threw Jonah overboard, the sea grew *calm* immediately!

At this the men greatly feared the LORD, and they offered a sacrifice to the LORD and made vows to him. JONAH 1:16

Jonah's disobedience was used by the LORD to spiritually save the sailors!

They *could* have been lost to the clutches of the Enemy, but the LORD GOD ALMIGHTY had mercy on them when they cried out to Him!

! PRAISE OUR LORD GOD
FOR HIS UNENDING MERCY!

Many situations do not end this way!

† Have *you* run from the LORD God…at any time in your life?
† Have *you* been disobedient to HIM?
† Have *you* repented for refusing to go where HE needed you to be?
† Have *you* ignored any request HE has asked of YOU…through the power of the Holy Spirit?
† Have *you* regretted any of His assignments? Then saw someone else take advantage of serving Him…and was *blessed* for it?

You see, dear one, there are **many** who come to ME! However, some stay until I **test** their *faithfulness* and *obedience*!

Following the Christ in thoughts, words, deeds, honesty and integrity and unconditional love, are the **MOST DIFFICULT ASSIGNMENTS** in your life…**unless** you continue to stay close to Me…and make Me first and foremost in your life!

♥ You do not become a Christ follower for WHAT I CAN GIVE YOU!
♥ You are a Christ follower for how much YOU CAN GIVE TO OTHERS!
♥ SERVING ME…in the smallest and the unseen tasks!
♥ SERVING ME…in loving those who take advantage of you!
♥ SERVING ME…in your service to others, who are thankless of what you do!

You can mop a floor, and do it with complete JOY, which will bring Glory to the Father!

You will find Me in the most mundane task!

Whether a task or assignment is important or not, YOU WILL FIND ME…only if your heart is steadfast on Me!

When I began to prepare Myself to wash the feet of My apostles, they did not pay attention to what I was doing!

Each was eating and laughing! They enjoyed each other's company! They had no idea what was going to happen that night!

The Sons of Thunder liked to entertain the others with stories of their Divine Encounters! Their laughter was heard throughout the house!

Thomas, of course, doubted some of their stories! However, he became angry when he told his stories and the others would pretend they did not believe him!

He traveled with Philip or Thaddeus, much of the time!

As I was filling the basin with water…I heard Philip denying what Thomas said!

"What? Oh Thomas...you exaggerate! None of that happened like you say!"

"Philip...you were right there! That man was crippled, and he dragged himself along the ground! Then, we prayed to the Father! We prayed in the name of the Master! Then the man got up and walked! He hopped, even! You were with me in Joppa!"

"Sorry, Thomas, I have no idea what you speak of! Joppa? We never even went there!"

At this, Philip winked at the others! The laughter roared and practically shook the plates and cups from the table!

When I started to wash their feet...the room became utterly quiet!

As I began to wash their feet, I prayed especially for that Apostle... knowing what each one would be facing, after I ascended into Heaven!

You do remember—when it was Peter's turn, do you not? He did not desire that I, the Master, do the task assigned to slaves! Peter did NOT understand what I was doing!

Jesus answered, "Unless I wash you, you have no part with me." JOHN 13:8

I then explained My desire to serve in this manner!

I set an example, not just for them, but for YOU reading or hearing these words, as well!

I tell you the truth, no servant is greater than his master, nor a messenger greater than the one who sent him. Now that you know these things, you will be blessed if you do them. JOHN 13:16-17

♥ Will YOU look for situations...to serve others?

♥ Will YOU take advantage of any opportunity I send your way?

♥ When you serve others...YOU ARE SERVING ME...the LORD of lords...the KING of kings!

...Taking your eyes off of yourself...

...Taking your mind away from yourself...

...Taking your love from yourself...

Is only **then**, that people will know you are one of My Divine Disciples!

Come! Pray with Me!

Come! Seek My Righteousness!

Come! Listen for the sounds of Angels' Wings!

I LOVE YOU WITH AN EVERLASTING LOVE
THAT COMES ONLY FROM ABOVE...
BEYOND MEASURE!

Christ, your Master,
Jesus

! PRAY AS I TAUGHT YOU !

"This, then, is how you should pray:
" 'Our Father in heaven,
hallowed be your name,
your kingdom come,
your will be done
on earth as it is in heaven.
Give us today our daily bread.
Forgive us our debts,
as we also have forgiven our debtors.
And lead us not into temptation,
but deliver us from the evil one.'
MATTHEW 6:9-13

O' My Most Precious Disciple,

The Father asks, "What do My people pray *for*? Why do My people *pray*?

- ♥ Do they pray the way that I taught them…through you, My Son?
- ♥ Do they pray for themselves…most of the time…or all of the time?
- ♥ Do they pray for others? Perhaps only close family members and friends?
- ♥ Do they pray for their enemies?

What do *they pray for*?

Why *do* they *pray*?"

"Words! So many words reach Me in Heaven! However, I still do not know what they are praying for, or for whom they are praying!

I tell you this, because many who pray…*pray amiss*! Tell them, again, My Son!"

Can you, dear one, visualize such a conversation between ABBA and Me?

I have left instructions on how you should pray! Perhaps you do not fully understand!

You are *My disciple*! Are you not?

Do you understand why the Father, our ABBA, asks such questions? It is not a mystery, dear one!

I speak to you, so that you may carry the message to others! Most of the time, the prayers are for themselves! Some of My followers **only pray** for themselves!

   ✝ Has the *world changed* because of the way *you prayed?*

   ✝ Has anything happened that is good because *you prayed?*

Yes! I hear PRAISES many times, and I am pleased!

However, those of you who know the importance of understanding prayer **must tell the others!**

Many times I hear the same requests over and over! However, many of those prayers are with selfish motives!

They are not praying according to My Will!

They may say those words; however, they go and control the situation or interfere with My perfect will!

   ✝ Why do My followers stand in the way of the Father's Perfect Will for those for whom they intercede?

Do you not know? I desire to do many things for you! When you pray to the Father, and you use My Name, I always answer!

Many times I answer quickly…and other times I must have you wait, because it is *My perfect will* for that particular prayer request! Do you understand?

   ✝ Look at the world about you!

…Step out of your 'personal cocoon'!

…See the pain that is going on around the world!

…Can you not *open* your *spiritual eyes* for just a moment…and lift others whom you do not know…who are suffering in a myriad of horrible ways…in prayer? Will you, dearest one?

   ✝ I must challenge you, dear followers! Tell My disciples to join you… in praying for others…for seven days! Yes! Only for others' needs— *not one request for yourselves!*

Will this be difficult? Yes…it will! Only if you have prayed *selfishly* in the past!

   * You must step out of your *circle!*

   * You must climb out of the *box!*

There is pain out there…spiritual pain, emotional pain, physical pain and financial pain!

For seven days, **pray for someone else and other situations, except your own!**

PRAISE Me!

WORSHIP Me!

ADORE Me!

Remember, I am a jealous God!
I yearn Praises from you!
I desire for your Worship!
I desire for you to Adore Me!
…Am I not your Creator?
…Am I not your Elohim?
…Am I not your Messiah?

Seek forgiveness! Offer thanksgiving from your heart! However, lift up another person or persons and other situations to Me and truly see what I will do!

- ♥ Pray with Faith!
- ♥ Pray with Hope!
- ♥ Pray with Joy!
- ♥ Pray with Belief!
- ♥ Pray the words that I taught My first disciples!

Do you realize that there are those who are risking their lives to bring My Word to people in countries that are very dangerous for them? They are imprisoned! They are tortured! Babies are being sold! Children are being taken!

- ~ There are those who are dying…many alone!
- ~ There are those who live in the streets!
- ~ There are those who are in need of love! And…no one to give it!

These are the things, and even more, which you should be praying about, when you gather together, or perhaps, when you go into your prayer closet!

You know what it says in My Word:

If you love those who love you, what reward will you get? Are not even the tax collectors doing that? And if you greet only your brothers, what are you doing more than others? Do not even the pagans do that? Be perfect, therefore, as your heavenly Father is perfect. MATTHEW 5:46-48

The Father hears!

Will you do this? You will be surprised at the burdens that will be lifted from your own shoulders, when you are yoked to Mine!

"Come to me, all you who are weary and burdened, and I will give you rest. Take my yoke upon you and learn from me, for I am gentle and humble in heart, and you will find rest for your souls. For my yoke is easy and my burden is light." MATTHEW 11:28-30

You must learn to let go and allow Me to work in the lives of your loved ones!

† Place them on My altar!

† Place them at the foot of My Cross! I will take care of them!

† You, as a disciple, must take care of My business!

The time is coming to an end!

Come! Sit with Me!

Come! Invoke the name of the Father…'Hallowed be thy name, dearest Father!'

Come! Sit with Me! Pray for your daily bread! Your spiritual bread! Protection, wisdom, discernment!

Do not think it was merely physical *food* I meant!

…*My bread* nourishes you beyond any food that the Earth has to offer!

…*My bread* fills you with joy and peace unending!

Come! Sit with Me! Seek forgiveness! Seek protection from the Enemy! Recognize his ploys! Do not be deceived!

Come! Sit with Me! Pray that all things are according to My will!

In Heaven, I speak a word, and it is done! Is this not what you desire on your Earth? My Perfect Will…'on *Earth* as it is in *Heaven*' ?

Come! Sit down with Me! Seek the Holy Spirit as to what and how you should pray!

!Listen for His voice!

…You are My beloved!

…You are My disciple!

…You are My extensions on Earth!

I have loved you since before the beginning of time …always beyond measure!

Come to Me! I will give you Living Water!

♥ I am your LORD!

♥ I am your KING!

♥ You are My CHOSEN!

♥ You are My BRIDE!

I Am THE CHRIST,
   Jesus

! DO YOU REALLY LOVE ME? !

*"At that time," declares the LORD, "I will be the God of
all the clans of Israel, and they will be my people."
This is what the LORD says:
"The people who survive the sword
will find favor in the desert;
I will come to give rest to Israel."
The LORD appeared to us in the past, saying:
"I have loved you with an everlasting love; I have drawn you with loving-
kindness. I will build you up again and you will be rebuilt, O Virgin Israel.
Again you will take up your tambourines and go out to dance with the joyful.
Again you will plant vineyards on the hills of Samaria; the farmers will plant
them and enjoy their fruit. There will be a day when watchmen cry out on
the hills of Ephraim, 'Come, let us go up to Zion, to the LORD our God.' "*
JEREMIAH 31:1-6

O' My Most Faithful Chosen People,

The LORD, your God, the Father and Creator of all, seeks your *unending love*!

The LORD, your God, the Almighty of the Universe, which He created, seeks your *unquestioning obedience*!

The LORD, your God, the Most High and Only True God, seeks your *unwavering trust*!

I speak to you of all the things, which the Father has given Me for you!

Therefore, I, the Son, of the Most High, ask you…His chosen among those of Israel and the Gentiles:

- *Do you love Me?* Then pick up your cross and follow ME!
- *Do you love Me?* Then stay on the narrow path…without looking to the right or to the left!
- *Do you love Me?* Then remain faithful!
- *Do you love Me?* Then forgive ALL who have hurt you!
- *Do you love Me?* Then give Me your grief, and sing out with JOY!
- *Do you love Me?* Then love those who have turned from you because of ME!
- *Do you love Me?* Then forgive yourself of past sins AND sin no more!
- *Do you love Me?* Then teach others of My Word!
- *Do you love Me?* Then hide NOT in your sin, nor in your grief;

illnesses; sadness; riches; poverty; pretenses; religiosity, not in your idolatry; nor dwell on the past!

Pray...as David did:

> *Who can discern his errors?*
> *Forgive my hidden faults.*
> *Keep your servant also from willful sins;*
> *may they not rule over me.*
> *Then will I be blameless,*
> *innocent of great transgression.*
> *May the words of my mouth*
> *and the meditation of my heart*
> *be pleasing in your sight.*
> *O LORD, my Rock and my Redeemer.*
> PSALM 19:12-14

Your lives, dearest ones, are an example of My love, and what I desire for you!

For I know the plans I have for you," declares the LORD, "plans to prosper you and not to harm you, plans to give you hope and a future. JEREMIAH 29:11

Have I, the LORD of lords, the KING of kings, not kept all the promises made to His chosen?

What have **you** done to keep the promises made during 'pleading prayer'?

Have you not sought Me with all your heart and soul?

Have I hidden from you?

Have I not heard you lift your voices toward the Heavens and promised thusly:

> *I seek you with all my heart;*
> *do not let me stray from your commands.*
> *I have hidden your word in my heart*
> *that I might not sin against you.*
> PSALM 119:10-11

I *desire* to believe you, My chosen ones, who are faithful and obedient!

Should I believe in *you*...as you believe in *Me*?

There is always hope...is there not?

† Are you, dear one, ready to stand away from the crowd? Even if there is a *'Jesus prophet' professing gospel lies to lead many astray?*

† Do you have the strength? This strength is NOT of the human kind!

41

† This strength comes only from your Master, the Christ!

Will you be 'broken bread' and 'poured out wine' for your Master, the LORD of lords?

I was…for **YOU**!

All the sins I have just mentioned …are just a fraction of a myriad of the sins…your sins…and those of your brothers and sisters…throughout the world!

These very sins kept Me *willingly* on the Cross!

I could have had My angels come to rescue Me! I only needed to say the word! However, I could NOT!

'WHY?' I hear you ask!

Because, My dearest, I *promised* the Heavenly Father, that I, His Only SON, would come to the Earth at His perfect timing to lift **His precious creation** from the clutches of the Enemy…Satan!

I promised Almighty God, EL GIBBOR, that the finality of My death on the Cross…and most importantly My Resurrection…would thwart the Enemy's plans FOREVER!

♥ Are you not *singing* with gladness?

♥ Are you not *praising* your Creator?

♥ Are you not *bowing* before GOD, JEHOVAH-nissi, your Victory?

♥ Are you not jumping for JOY with the angels in Heaven?

Most of you have missed the Joyous Resurrection Celebration!

However, put a smile on your face…go out and share this most wondrous, most blessed, and the most mysterious promise made…**AND** fulfilled!

Now…look up!

You will NOT miss the most Glorious Event!

"At that time the sign of the Son of Man will appear in the sky, and all the nations of the earth will mourn. They will see the Son of Man coming on the clouds of the sky, with power and great glory. And he will send his angels with a loud trumpet call, and they will gather his elect from the four winds, from one end of the heavens to the other. MATTHEW 24:30-31

So I say to you, again, O precious of My Father, LOOK UP!

I, your Savior, will return and take you to be with Me…FOREVER!

† **BE SPIRITUALLY ALERT**!

Come! Take hold of the Savior's hand!

Come! Listen for your Master's voice!

Come! Answer the call!

Come! Meet Me in the clouds!

Oh, My Beloved! The Father is preparing for this Great and Glorious Day!

Never forget: I, the LORD of lords…

LOVED YOU BEFORE THE BEGINNING OF TIME!

♥ **YOU ARE MINE!**

♥ **I AM YOURS!**

I AM…THE CHRIST,

Jesus

! WHERE ARE YOUR ACCUSERS !

"I tell you the truth, whoever hears my word and believes him who sent me has eternal life and will not be condemned; he has crossed over from death to life. I tell you the truth, a time is coming and has now come when the dead will hear the voice of the Son of God and those who hear will live. For as the Father has life in himself, so he has granted the Son to have life in himself. And he has given him authority to judge because he is the Son of Man. "Do not be amazed at this, for a time is coming when all who are in their graves will hear his voice and come out—those who have done good will rise to live, and those who have done evil will rise to be condemned. By myself I can do nothing; I judge only as I hear, and my judgment is just, for I seek not to please myself but him who sent me.
JOHN 5:24-30

O' My Cherished Disciples,

Seeking forgiveness is what the Father desires from His sons and His daughters!

✝ Have you not *desired* to be *spent* for Me?

✝ Have you not *experienced* the *crushing* of your heart?

✝ Have you not felt the *tearing apart* of your very *spirit*…of your *soul*…that your *mind* is unable to understand?

AM I NOT JEHOVAH-rophe…your Healer?

✝ Have you not felt *loneliness*?

AM I NOT JEHOVAH-shammah…with you wherever you are?

✝ Have you not felt all *alone…abandoned*?

AM I NOT JEHOVAH-rohi…your Shepherd?

✝ Have I not *promised* that I will never leave you, nor forsake you?

AM I NOT JEHOVAH-shalom…your Peace?

O friend! What do you *desire* to do in the Name of JESUS?

…Is it according to the Will of the Father?

THEN IT WILL BE DONE!

O friend! When your *pain* in the world is great…will you not believe that My LOVE…My JOY…My HOPE…My PEACE…are greater?

THEN YOU WILL HAVE THEM!

✝ Have you *forgiven* others, as I have forgiven you?

✝ Have you *loved unconditionally*, as I have loved you?

O dear son! O dearest daughter!

* Have you not *comforted* others, with the comfort you have received?
* Have you not *prayed* for the sick and dying?
* Have you not *fed* the hungry, or given a *drink* to the thirsty?

THEN YOU HAVE DONE ALL UNTO ME!

ABBA, GOD Almighty, will *never* forget anything you have done, in the Name of His only Begotten SON!

Though your sins are many...they are forgiven...and forgotten...when you accept JESUS of Nazareth...as your SAVIOR...become filled with the HOLY SPIRIT...and are BORN-AGAIN!

♥ You were born of water...
   ♥ Now you are born of the Spirit!
♥ You followed those in the world...
   ♥ Now you desire to follow Me!

Therefore, cherished disciple, look **not** to the right, **nor** to the left, **nor** behind you!

Keep your eyes on Me!

Listen only for My Voice!

Those who *accuse* you falsely, because of Me, are from the Enemy's 'campground'!

They will be bound and thrown into the pit of fire forever...unless they repent of their sins and accept Me as their LORD and Savior!

♥ And you, My son, and you, My daughter...WILL LIVE IN PARADISE, with Me...the LORD of lords...for Eternity!!

I tell you the Truth...there is much to be done, that only you, hearing or reading these words, are being equipped to accomplish!

I need the *heart* that has been broken...and the *spirit* that has been crushed...so I can *remold* and *reshape* you into a most beautiful creation for ABBA!

♥ PRAISE ME...for allowing your *heart* to be broken!
♥ ADORE ME...when your *spirit* feels crushed!
♥ WORSHIP ME...when your *soul* is in anguish!

Through all of these experiences...your LORD has been preparing to use you in the lives of many...who are waiting for the Master to accomplish ABBA's 'perfect will' in their lives!

You, precious disciple, are needed to extend My LOVE...My JOY... My PEACE...and My ANOINTING on those whose *hearts are being made ready* by the HOLY SPIRIT!

Because of your unwavering faithfulness and obedience...you have been chosen to *plant* or to *water* the spiritual seeds in these hearts!

♥ Wherever you are…I will use you!

♥ Wherever you go…I will lead you!

Yes! O blessed disciple…you may be in prison; or in hospital; in an orphanage; or on the battlefield; in the work-place; or at home, caring for your family; or giving your time to help the poor and the homeless; or perhaps you are a servant in homes of the rich and famous; even on a bed, because you are suffering pain throughout your body; or you could be facing death!

♥ Whatever the situation…your Divine Assignment is always Intercessory Prayer!

♥ LOOK UP…for Heaven is always before you!

Remember what happened to the woman who was caught in adultery? She was dragged from her house, and brought before Me!

The teachers of the Law and the Pharisees, who came to Me…accusing her…demanded for her to be stoned to death…as was written in the Law of Moses!

I am telling you this…so you will always remember to **fear GOD more than man!**

We were in the temple courts…when a crowd of men brought the woman before Me!

They were using this situation to trap Me…in order to have a reason to accuse Me!

When they kept on questioning him, he straightened up and said to them, "If any one of you is without sin, let him be the first to throw a stone at her." Again he stooped down and wrote on the ground.

At this, those who heard began to go away one at a time, the older ones first, until only Jesus was left, with the woman standing there. Jesus straightened up and asked her, "Woman, where are they? Has no one condemned you?"

"No one sir," she said.

"Then neither do I condemn you," Jesus declared. "Go now and leave your life of sin." JOHN 8:7-11

† HEAVEN OR HELL…a choice each one must make for their Eternal Life after their Temporary Life is over!

Therefore, I say to all who accept Me, on Earth…will Live in Eternity in Heaven!

~ Remain in My Light!

~ Step into My Shadow!

~ Be filled with My Joy!

~ Come boldly into the Throne Room!

!BE NOT AFRAID!

Therefore, there is now no condemnation for those who are in Christ Jesus, because through Christ Jesus the law of the Spirit of life set me free from the law of sin and death. ROMANS 8:1-2

You, beloved disciple, belong to **Me**...and to Me alone...because you have answered the call of the LORD of lords!

♥ I AM THE LIGHT OF THE WORLD!

✝ I AM JESUS WHO DIED FOR YOU!

♥ I AM THE SAVIOR WHOM YOU LOVE...
AND HE WHO LOVES YOU...BEYOND MEASURE!

Your Friend Forever,
  Yeshua ha'Machiach

! WHO IS IN YOUR FAMILY? !

This is how the birth of Jesus Christ came about: His mother Mary was pledged to be married to Joseph, but before they came together, she was found to be with child through the Holy Spirit. Because Joseph her husband was a righteous man and did not want to expose her to public disgrace, he had in mind to divorce her quietly. But after he had considered this, an angel of the Lord appeared to him in a dream and said, "Joseph son of David, do not be afraid to take Mary home as your wife, because what is conceived in her is from the Holy Spirit. She will give birth to a son, and you are to give him the name Jesus, because he will save his people from their sins."
MATTHEW 1:18-21

O' My Most Precious Disciple,

What of you...have you understood what I have asked of you...in your Divine Assignments?

Is the question not always before you, in these last days?

Just as Joseph, and Jeremiah, Noah, and Moses...and the many prophets then and now...have been given Blessed work to accomplish for the LORD GOD...so are you, reading or hearing these messages!

My answers are understood by those who are filled with the HOLY SPIRIT!

Are you pleased with your LORD's answer, or has this not *confused* many people?

Remember, any and all confusion is not from EL GIBBOR—GOD Almighty!

The world in which you live is governed by the Enemy...yours and Ours!

Satan and his cohorts delight in twisting the Inspired Words of the LORD GOD!

Never forget...he was also *created* by ELOHIM!

The first sin was of Pride!

Before the beginning of time, as you know it...Lucifer and all who desired to follow him...were cast from Paradise...which was created for Us and Our Angels!

He went to the Earth, and became that world's god...along with the angels who decided to follow him, because they were given a Free Will!

The Father—GOD Almighty—the I AM WHO AM—set the day

and time for sending His only begotten Son...to be born of a virgin...and become the most pure and final Blood Sacrifice...to save Our people from their sin!

All this took place to fulfill what the Lord had said through the prophet: "the virgin will be with child and will give birth to a son, and they will call him Immanuel"—which means, "God with us."

When Joseph woke up, he did what the angel of the Lord had commanded him and took Mary home as his wife. But he had no union with her until she gave birth to a son. And he gave him the name Jesus. MATTHEW 1:22-25

At the *perfect time* – as are **all** things which the LORD GOD Almighty has and does plan – He sent Me out to begin My Divine Assignment!

I left My earthly family and friends, and went to the Jordan, to be baptized by My cousin, John!

But John tried to deter him, saying, "I need to be baptized by you, and do you come to me?"

Jesus replied, "Let it be so now; it is proper for us to do this to fulfill all righteousness." Then John consented. MATTHEW 3:14-15

My cousin, John, was a humble man...he was *compelled* to accomplish *his* Divine Assignment, as well!

What of you, dear disciple?

Is any thing or any one keeping you from obeying the Voice of your LORD Redeemer?

As soon as I was baptized, I went up out of the water! There were many men and women waiting patiently to be baptized by John!

At the moment I came out of the water, I saw the Spirit of GOD descending like a dove and was lighting on Me!

And a voice from heaven said, "This is my Son, whom I love; with him I am well pleased." MATTHEW 3:17

Does your heart and spirit not feel the joy to hear words like these from an earthly parent?

Many of you *have not* and *will not* experience this most profound *declaration* of unconditional love from an earthly parent!

However, dear and precious disciple, open your *spiritual ears* and hear the Voice of the One Who created you!

Come closer to Adonai, and learn of ELOHIM's great love for you!

Draw nigh unto ABBA...for He will draw nigh unto you, His beloved child!

The Voice of the LORD of lords...the GOD of gods...calls your name and desires for you to come into HIS PRESENCE each day and night!

Have you not understood?

Have you not heard?

Have you not seen?

You, dearest disciple, have been born into the most perfect and greatest family any one could ever hope for, on the Earth AND in Heaven!

- ♥ I, JESUS of Nazareth, am your BROTHER!
- ♥ WE, dear heart, share the same FATHER!
- ♥ YOU, blessed one, ARE A CHILD OF THE KING of kings!
- ♥ YOU, cherished disciple, ARE in the Family of the Most High GOD!
- ♥ YOU, beloved child, ARE a Royal Priesthood…

among Our chosen people, and within a HOLY NATION!

…, a people belonging to God, that you may declare the praises of him who called you out of darkness into his wonderful light. Once you were not a people, but now you are the people of God; once you had not received mercy, but now you have received mercy. 1 PETER 2:9-10

- † How does your *heart* react to know that you, dearest, are in the Family of the LIVING GOD?
- † What of your *mind?*

    …Too much to *comprehend?*

    …Too much to be able to *truly believe,* or *understand?*

- † What of your *spirit?*

    …Too much *joy* that leaves you *speechless* and in *awe?*

    …Too much *gladness* that has you *desire* to sing out 'PRAISE THE LORD' wherever you may be at any moment…regardless of who may hear you?

- † What of your *soul?*

    …Too much *peace* that surpasses human understanding, to truly *know* that your heart, mind, spirit and soul will *live forever* in the Presence of the KING of kings?

Therefore, do you remember what I said to someone who told Me that My mother and brothers were standing outside to speak to Me?

He replied to him, "Who is my mother, and who are my brothers?" Pointing to his disciples, he said, "Here are my mother and my brothers. For whoever does the will of My Father in heaven is my brother and sister and mother." MATTHEW 12:48-50

Are you, dear disciple, desiring to do the will of the Father – GOD ALMIGHTY – which is HIS PERFECT WILL for Our true followers?

This is why I responded as I did!

Your Savior was not ignoring the fact that My earthly family had come to see Me!

I took the blessed opportunity to make My Father's teaching known to all who were within hearing that day!

This comment of Mine was quickly spread throughout to Jews and Gentiles, alike!

Does this not please and bless you, dear friend?

My earthly family, other than Mary, My earthly mother, did not always understand My words or actions!

A few followed Me, without questioning!

All believed in Me, **after** My death on the Cross and My Resurrection!

Are you able to even imagine their reactions, and those of the others, when I *appeared* to them...unannounced?

A surprise to believers...that I would even think of them!

A shock to those who had many doubts, that the Son of Man...was *actually* the only begotten SON of GOD...fulfilling all prophecies of the coming of the MESSIAH!

- ♥ Therefore, My beloved brother, My precious sister...you have been chosen to receive My messages through today's willing and available scribes!
- ♥ I am speaking to Our faithful and obedient friends and followers... in these last days...as I have from the beginning!
- ♥ Seek *discernment* from the Blessed Scriptures, and *Spiritual Insight* from the HOLY SPIRIT...always, dear one!

Come...rest and listen for My Voice!

Come...you are family in the House of GOD Most High...the Almighty and True!

Come...Our door is always open to believing family and friends!

YOU, BELOVED FAMILY,
ARE LOVED BEYOND MEASURE!

Your Brother Forever,
   Yeshua ha'Machiach

You are Divinely Invited To Attend:

Eternal Life Celebration

Master of Ceremonies

JESUS THE CHRIST

Place: HEAVEN

Date/Time: WHEN YOU ARE CALLED!

COMPLIMENTS OF THE HOST:

7 Star Accomodations

Gourmet Meals / Life Giving Waters

Dancing / Dining

Live Music Povided by:

The Angelic Choir

All Expenses paid in full by:

The Blood of the Lamb

COME CELEBRATE!!!

In The Kingdom of Our God!

R.S.V.P. WHILE THERE IS STILL TIME!

! GLORIFY THE FATHER FIRST !

*"You believe at last!" Jesus answered. "But a time is coming, and has
come, when you will be scattered, each to his own home. You will
leave me alone. Yet I am not alone, for my Father is with me.
"I have told you these things, so that in me you may have peace. In this
world you will have trouble. But take heart! I have overcome the world."
After Jesus said this, he looked toward heaven and prayed: "Father, the time
has come. Glorify your Son, that your Son may glorify you. For you granted
him authority over all people that he might give eternal life to all those you
have given him. Now this is eternal life: that they may know you, the only
true God, and Jesus Christ, whom you have sent. I have brought you glory
on earth by completing the work you gave me to do. And now, Father, glorify
me in your presence with the glory I had with you before the world began.*
JOHN 16:31 – 17:4-5

O' My Most Faithful and Obedient Disciple,

The Father knows how much you have PRAISED and WORSHIPED
the SON!

He knows how much you have THANKED and BLESSED Him with
your acts of ADORATION!

However, I, the SON of OUR MOST HIGH and ALMIGHTY
GOD, must continue to remind *all* My disciples, to remember to live your
lives in ways to bring **Him** the Glory, which He deserves AND desires!

*So whether you eat or drink or whatever you do, do it all for the glory of
God.* 1 CORINTHIANS 10:31

You **must** have this attitude in your mind…first and foremost!

♥ Seek the control of the Holy Spirit!

♥ Your mind will direct how you *act* and *react* through any
circumstance!

♥ Put on the Mind of Christ in all you do and say!

Remember: others, especially non-believers, are watching you very
closely, if you *profess* to belong to the Christ!

*Do not cause anyone to stumble, whether Jews, Greeks or the church of
God—even as I try to please everybody in every way. For I am not seeking my own
good but the good of many, so that they may be saved. …* 1 CORINTHIANS
10:32-33

These inspired words…from the HOLY SPIRIT…were written to the people of the church at Corinth through My Apostle, Paul!

Paul was living an empty existence! Empty, because he did NOT have the knowledge of the CHRIST and HIM CRUCIFIED! His mind did NOT—could NOT—comprehend this mystery! Therefore, he persecuted the people who loved our Most High GOD…and believed in the SON of GOD!

It was not until Paul's total transformation…from Saul to Paul…that he lived to give Glory to the Father!

As his mind tried to grasp the truth of the Christ, his heart was turning from a *'heart of stone to a heart of flesh'*…filled no longer with hate, but with Divine Love!

He decided to *surrender his soul* to the Risen Christ, JESUS!

He then lived to save God's people by *preaching* the Truth!

And what of you, dearest one?

?Are YOU *putting* on the Mind and Heart of Christ?

?Are YOU allowing your heart and soul to be *guided* by the Holy Spirit?

…Turn to Me…so that others will also *see* Divine Love!

…Turn to Me…so that Peace will *shine* on your face!

…Turn to Me…so that others will *desire* the Joy that will radiate through your eyes!

…Turn to Me…so that you will *remember* the radiance of those who have gone before you!

…Turn to Me…so that you will *share* in My Cross… *willingly* and *gratefully*!

…Turn to Me…so that you will have *discernment* as to know those who still have the *veil* covering their faces…as Moses said long ago…and still to this day!

A *veil* covers the faces of those who have NOT given themselves freely to CHRIST, Crucified!

…Turn to Me…so that others will *wonder* as to why *you see* clearly… because the *veil* has been removed…and now understand!

Now the Lord is the Spirit, and where the Spirit of the Lord is, there is freedom. And we, who with unveiled faces all reflect the Lord's glory, are being transformed into his likeness with ever-increasing glory, which comes from the Lord, who is the Spirit. 2 CORINTHIANS 3:17-18

+ It is good to *learn* about My Word!
+ It is better to *understand* what it is I am truly saying!

- It is best to seek the wisdom, knowledge and discernment that is being imparted through the Holy Spirit!

When do you yearn to give Glory to the Father?

…Is it when you are suffering, as My friend, Job, did?

…Is it only when you are living a 'mountaintop experience'?

Your very existence is to bring Glory to GOD!

Have you, dearest disciple, ever grasped this truth?

Not every disciple has! This is what saddens the Father…the Creator of your being and your very soul!

Therefore…live to give Him Glory…in all you *think*, in all you *love*, in all you *do*, and even when you are at *rest*!

† Offer a Sacrifice of GLORY, PRAISE, WORSHIP, and ADORATION in and for ALL circumstances!

    …In JOY!

      …In PAIN!

        …In SICKNESS!

        …In HEALTH!

Make these words of David…your prayer:

Teach me your way, O LORD, and I will walk in your truth; give me an undivided heart, that I may fear your name. PSALM 86:11

You are My beloved!

I AM WHO AM…
THE ONE AND ONLY GOD OF GLORY!
I LOVE YOU ABOVE AND BEYOND MEASURE!

Yeshua ha'Machiach

Precious Sweet-one:

The Son is the radiance of God's glory and the exact representation of his being, sustaining all things by his powerful word. After he had provided purification for sins, he sat down at the right hand of the Majesty in heaven.
HEBREWS 1:3

! LOOK ONLY UNTO ME !

Brothers, I do not consider myself yet to have taken hold of it. But one thing I do: Forgetting what is behind and straining toward what is ahead, I press on toward the goal to win the prize for which God has called me heavenward in Christ Jesus. All of us who are mature should take such a view of things. And if on some point you think differently, that too God will make clear to you. Only let us live up to what we have already attained.
PHILIPPIANS 3:13-16

O' My Dearest Disciples,

Do you find it strange that you are experiencing some of what My friend Job experienced?

Do you doubt My *love*?

Do you think I have *abandoned* you?

Do you doubt My *forgiveness*?

† **I would not have died on the Cross, if I did not love you!**

I must remind you of words that I have said to you before! When things are assaulting you, look not to the right, nor to the left, and do not turn around! You must *look forward* and *look up*!

One day, very soon, you will see Me coming to remove you from this Earth!

Remember…I am *greater* because *I* fill your heart!

You, dear children, are from God and have overcome them, because the one who is in you is greater than the one who is in the world. 1 JOHN 4:4

♥ Have you asked Me to fill your heart, dear one, *completely*?

♥ Have you been joyful to *accept* whatever *My will* is for you?

Be not afraid! I promised I would be with you always…forever!

I must tell you…you cannot expect everyone to understand what you have learned! It is because of your *personal walk* with Me! The more difficult the walk, the closer you come to Me! This is as it should be! Is it not?

Yes, there are those who still remain in spiritual darkness! However, you, My dearest disciple, must continue to walk towards the Light!

Am I not the Light? I must be *everything* to you!

* What does it mean to you that you have been *saved by* GRACE?

…Have you never shown *grace* to someone?

…Fed a hungry person?

…Given out of your own need?

…Have you not said kind words to someone who was hurting?

The more you are filled with My Grace and Mercy…the more will spill over into the lives of others!

There are those among you, who desire more of My Grace…who desire more from Me!

Do you not see how many among you, hold Me at *arms length*? I do not speak of the unbelievers…I speak of those who claim they are part of the Body of Christ!

They draw near to Me…only when they are in need…then I am forgotten…until the next time! Then they wonder why they do not have a closer walk with Me! FOOLS – they are FOOLS!

He who trusts in himself is a fool, but he who walks in wisdom is kept safe. PROVERBS 28:26

When you are in pain…whether it be of the spirit, the mind, the heart, or the soul…even the body…and you recognize the pain I suffered for you… then you will understand what it is to be *Crucified with the Christ*!

The more you are available to Me, the closer we become! This is why I call you *friend*!

When you experience any sorrow which Job experienced…then you are *learning* what it is to be *Crucified with Me*!

It must be this way, dearest one! I know you do not understand this now, but one day you will see all clearly!

I love you! Did I not love Job? Does not a mother *chastise* her child because of her love for that child? It is even more important for your LORD to *chastise* those He loves! To draw them closer!

♥ Be not afraid! You must learn from Me, how to bring your mind into a peaceful state! You must allow your heart…that same peace!

Remember…the mind is the Devil's playground! It is important for you to pray protection and plead My Blood upon your mind every day! Even all day and into the night! This *spiritual battle* is one of the greatest battles you will encounter!

Put on the full armor of God so that you can take your stand against the devil's schemes. EPHESIANS 6:11

♥ Be not afraid! Stand in My Shadow…so I will be facing the Enemy… not you!

Look…My arms are raised!

Look…My sleeves flow wider from My outstretched arms…protecting you even more!

Do not be fooled by *false spirits*! You must seek *spiritual insight*! When you meet someone with a false spirit, cry out to Me!

For our struggle is not against flesh and blood, but against the rulers, against the authorities, against the powers of this dark world and against the spiritual forces of evil in the heavenly realms. EPHESIANS 6:12

✝ Remember…there is power in My Name…JESUS!

✝ Remember…to Whom you belong!

✝ Am I not JESUS…your LORD? Do not be embarrassed to say it!

Do all to the Glory of the Father in the power of the Holy Spirit!

In My Name, JESUS, the Father will grant you anything according to His perfect will! Seek to know His perfect will!

When you find yourself in a situation that is too difficult to bear, cover yourself with the Blood of the LAMB of GOD!

Ask for My Warrior Angels to surround you!

There is nothing you cannot do when you believe and trust, in the Father's perfect will!

Come! My chosen one!

Come! Feel My arms around you!

Come! The time is short!

Work diligently on any Assignment that I give you!

Discern which 'encounters' are from Me!

Praise Me for the Divine Delays!

Ask Me for My Divine Intervention…in difficult situations!

I would not speak to you thusly, if you were not chosen—if I did not love you—*of which there is no doubt*, because **I died for you**!

♥ NOW GO…

…Be filled with My *Peace*!

…Be filled with My *Joy*!

…Be covered with My *Blood*!

Always remember…the LORD of lords…the KING of kings…Loves You, dear disciple, Beyond Measure!

I am *Jesus*, the Christ, Who speaks to *you*!

! ARE YOU A HYPOCRITE? !

In the same way, on the outside you appear to people as righteous but on the inside you are full of hypocrisy and wickedness.
MATTHEW 23:28

O' My Dear Followers,

So many of you *profess* to *know* Me! Think again! Do you really *know* Me…your LORD…or…only *of* Me?

So many of you say you desire to do My Perfect will! However, it is not *My* will…*it is yours!* And this 'will' is not 'perfect' by any means!

Why? Why do you tell others that you are a follower of the Christ? Is this not being heartless to those who do not know Me? IT IS! It is truly being heartless! Do you know why? It is because they *watch you*, and the things that you do, and wonder: 'Is this all I have to do to follow JESUS… called the Christ…and be called a *Christian?*'

How can I call you a *true* follower? **Who** are you following? It certainly is not Me! The LORD of lords! The KING of kings!

† Do any among you understand what it *truly means* to follow your LORD?

† Do any among you understand what it *truly means* to be the son or the daughter of Our Most High GOD?

† Do any among you understand what it truly means to be a *follower* of the Christ? The Christ…Who **died for you?**

…Is your heart filled with sadness at My death?

…Is your heart filled with JOY at My Resurrection?

…You must answer 'NO'! You *must* answer 'NO'!

You are leading others astray…other men and women! And worse… are the children! The young children! The little children! They are watching you! How can they come to Me when they see the things that you do?

You lie…do you not? You call it a 'white lie' and 'white lies' do not count! Is this not what you tell yourselves?

Do not lie to each other, since you have taken off your old self with its practices and have put on the new self, which is being renewed in knowledge in the image of its Creator. COLOSSIANS 3:9-10

You cheat! You cheat on your taxes!

Tell us then, what is your opinion? Is it right to pay taxes to Caesar or not?"

But Jesus, knowing their evil intent, said, "You hypocrites, why are you trying to trap me? Show me the coin used for paying the tax." They brought him a denarius, and he asked them, "Whose portrait is this? And whose inscription?"

"Caesar's," they replied.

Then he said to them, "Give to Caesar what is Caesar's, and to God what is God's."

When they heard this, they were amazed. So they left him and went away. MATTHEW 22:17-21

You speak out profane words, then say, *"Oh, the Lord does not mind!* He knows how angry I am at that person, so that word or those words do not count! He knows me! He knows I love Him!"

Do others truly know that *you* love the Christ…through your sinful actions and reactions?

Are My disciples being *genuine witnesses* of the SON of GOD?

*"Do not follow the crowd in doing wrong. …*EXODUS 23:2

However, there are still consequences to your sins!

There are many instances where you lie! Think about them! Does this bring remorse? Does this mean you will stop and say only the truth?

When someone asks you to visit them, what do you say? "Oh, sorry! I cannot come right now! I have another pressing engagement?" But you do not! You do not want to go and see that particular person! You lie, and think it is alright!

Are you not being *heartless?*

I could mention many instances; however, I will let you think on these!

O My dear people…My true followers desire to emulate Me, the Christ!

- ♥ I am humble of heart!
- ♥ I am gentle of spirit!
- ♥ I have forgiven each of you!

Therefore, as God's chosen people, holy and dearly loved, clothe yourselves with compassion, kindness, humility, gentleness and patience. Bear with each other and forgive whatever grievances you may have against one another. Forgive as the Lord forgave you. And over all these virtues put on love, which binds them all together in perfect unity. COLOSSIANS 3:12-14

- † Have you not heard of why I died for you?
- † Have you not heard of all the sins…

…That caused me to be beaten and beaten with 39 lashes which tore at My flesh?

…That placed a Crown of Thorns upon My head?

…That nailed My hands and feet?

…That kept me on the Cross?

† Did I do this for you, O sinner?

YES…I did it for *EACH* OF YOU!

You make excuses! When an excuse is not necessary! Then you come, and seek forgiveness, and say to Me, 'I am sorry, LORD! I did not know that those *white lies* were sins!'

O sinner! Please do not insult the intelligence of your God!

My followers work hard to set their minds…their hearts…their spirits… their very souls to following Me! And following in My footsteps means they try hard *not* to sin! Not big sins…not little sins…not white lies!

But I say to you…a sin is a sin!

† Are you not afraid of Judgment Day?

† Are you not afraid that you may end up in eternal damnation?

† Are you not afraid, that the children who see you lie and cheat will think it is alright…and emulate *you*…and will not accept the Free Gift of Salvation…and end up in Hell which was created for Satan and his evil followers?

For we must all appear before the judgment seat of Christ, that each one may receive what is due him for the things done while in the body, whether good or bad. 2 CORINTHIANS 5:10

♥ Your heart must be filled with My love!

♥ Your heart must be filled with the desire to sin no more!

…It was your sin that kept Me on the Cross!

…It was your sin that nailed Me to that Cross!

† The Father weeps to see His creation reject Me and My love!

† The Father weeps to see His creation abandon…with heartlessness… the Son He sent to die for you!

Do you not believe this?

Do you not understand I can send you to eternal torment…if you continue on your path?

Those of you who follow Me, the LORD of lords, the KING of kings… will find it very difficult to live in this world…when your heart is filled with Love and Forgiveness…with Trust and Truth…and be surrounded with those whose hearts have love only for themselves!

The Father weeps when women who find themselves with child, then refuse to have that child…and *kill it*! Do you not understand? And women are not the only ones responsible…but the men who give no thought to consequences of their own pleasures! That *child* is a person with a SOUL and who was never given an opportunity to live and fulfill My perfect will!

O dear people!

...*Wars* are caused because of greed!

...*Tortures* are done because the Enemy has taken hold of men's hearts and minds...a complete hold...and men allow Satan to use them!

The Lord is not slow in keeping his promise, as some understand slowness. He is patient with you, not wanting anyone to perish, but everyone to come to repentance. 2 PETER 3:9

- ♥ There are those who have been *telling* you about Me!
- ♥ There are those who *pray* for all souls!
- ♥ There are those who *love* and *forgive* in My Name!
- ♥ Their hearts are filled with *unconditional love*...

with peace that surpasses human understanding! Would you not like to have this?

Come! Allow Me to anoint you!

Come! Allow Me to bless you!

Come! Allow Me to lead you into righteousness!

Come! Be not afraid! I am JESUS Who invites you to become My follower...

...My disciple!

...My friend!

...My beloved!

Have you not known...have you not seen...have you

not heard...the God who created you...

Loves You Beyond Measure?

I love you...and **My Love Is Pure!**

♥ I LOVE YOU! ♥

I Am the Christ,
  Yeshua!

! SCOFFER...OR WISE FOOL? !

The fear of the LORD is the beginning of wisdom; all
who follow his precepts have good understanding.
To him belongs eternal praise.
PSALM 111:10

The fool says in his heart, "There is no God."
PSALM 14:1

Fools mock at making amends for sin,
but goodwill is found among the upright.
PROVERBS 14:9

First of all, you must understand that in the last days scoffers
will come, scoffing and following their own desires.
2 PETER 3:3

O' My Faithful and Obedient Disciple,

My messages, which have been written...and are still being written... are to be taken as **truth** from your **Sovereign LORD**!

Do not ever think, that I, the LORD of lords...the KING of kings, have stopped communicating through those who have been chosen; and who have given themselves over for ALMIGHTY GOD's purposes!

I have NEVER stopped speaking through My chosen men and women!

Just as I chose My first apostles and disciples...these chosen have given themselves over completely to ME...through much *prayer and personal suffering*!

These chosen have spent much time in *lonely listening*!

If anyone of My chosen is reading or hearing these words...at this very moment...then you are filled with understanding from the depths of your heart...your soul...your mind...your spirit!

I, your LORD, ask you to pray and intercede for the others who will read or hear these words and SCOFF...as is their usual way!

However, no more!

Time...as you know it...is running out!

There **must** be a **great revival** around the Earth!

There are too many who are living their lives *only* for what they can gain for themselves!

But for you who revere my name, the sun of righteousness will rise with healing in its wings. And you will go out and leap like calves released from the stall. MALACHI 4:2

Think of what YOU are trying to do for the Kingdom! It is becoming more and more difficult to have people even try to listen to the Truth, is it not?

Too many people on the Earth…would rather NOT hear any truth… so as not to interfere with their selfish lives!…with their idols!…with their false gods!

I tell you, dearest disciple, gather your brothers and sisters! Say to them, '**WAKE UP, O PEOPLE**'!

All that has been and still is predicted, WILL come to pass!

First of all, you must understand, that in the last days, scoffers will come…following their own evil desires!

They will say,

"Where is this 'coming' he promised? Ever since our fathers died, everything goes on as it has since the beginning of creation." But they deliberately forget that long ago by God's word the heavens existed and the earth was formed out of water and by water. 2 PETER 3:4-5

The other thing is, dear one, these same waters deluged the earth and destroyed the world!

What they do not understand, is that by the same WORD…the present heavens and earth are reserved for fire…waiting for the Day of Judgment and destruction…to rid from the LORD's sight…all ungodly men and women!

But do not forget this one thing dear friends:

With the Lord a day is like a thousand years, and a thousand years are like a day. The Lord is not slow in keeping his promise, as some understand slowness. He is patient with you, not wanting anyone to perish, but everyone to come to repentance. 2 PETER 3:8-9

Our Omnipotent and Glorious God Almighty…desires for every one to come to repentance!

…Have you not told them?

…Have you not spread the Word?

…Have you not shouted the Truth?

"For God so loved the world that he gave his one and only Son, that whoever believes in him shall not perish but have eternal life. For God did not send his Son into the world to condemn the world, but to save the world through him. JOHN 3:16-17

This should be the most wonderful news...anyone...anywhere...would desire to embrace!

Just the IDEA that any one...any where...any sinner... just has to BELIEVE in the SON OF GOD...as the SAVIOR...just BELIEVE... and he or she...WILL BE SAVED!

Imagine...*understanding*...they will live **forever and ever and ever**...to no end...in the presence of **God Almighty...forever and ever and ever**!

† **LIFE**: Rewards of Heaven!

† **DEATH**: Punishment of Hell!

Tell the other disciples to spread the Word...the most wonderful and beautiful Word: '**Being Saved Does NOT Hurt...It HEALS!**'

Now, dear one, bow your head...that I may give you an extra anointing!

You will need much strength to do ALL, I, your Master, have for you... in order to accomplish your individual Divine Assignments!

Come! Be **covered** by My Blood!

Come! Be **clad** with the Armor of the Holy Spirit!

Come! Be **discerning** which spirit is of Me...and which is of Satan... OUR ENEMY!

♥ Remember: never neglect praying...for and with each other!

♥ Remember: spend time with Me...before you begin each day!

♥ Remember: speak with Me...before you go to sleep!

**I AM WHO AM...LOVES YOU WHO ARE...
BEYOND MEASURE!
I WILL NEVER LEAVE YOU,
NOR FORSAKE YOU!**

The Master...your Friend,
   Jesus

Precious Sweet-one:

But God chose the foolish things of the world to shame the wise; God chose the weak things of the world to shame the strong. He chose the lowly things of this world and the despised things—and the things that are not—to nullify the things that are, so that no one may boast before him.
1 CORINTHIANS 1:27-29

! WHATEVER I DID
...YOU WILL DO...
AND MORE !

Then Peter came to Jesus and asked, "Lord, how many times shall I forgive my brother when he sins against me? Up to seven times?" Jesus answered, "I tell you, not seven times, but seventy-seven times.
MATTHEW 18:21-22

O' My Most Precious Disciples,

- ♥ How long have you been following after Me?
- ♥ How many times have you sinned?
- ♥ How many times have you 'fretted' over those who have hurt you... whether deliberately or by an error in human judgment?
- ♥ How many times have you done the exact same thing to someone else?

Do you understand this?

If you do, then quickly go to that person and make peace! **Seek forgiveness**! Greet each other with a *Holy kiss*!

Then return and continue to follow ME...the MESSIAH!

Ask yourself: 'Why do I follow this Man?'

This Man...'Who says He is the Promised Messiah?'

Pray to understand what makes you *different* from the Chief Priests, the Pharisees, the Sadducees, the Rabbis, the Sanhedrin...who *know* the Law! And all those others, who *think* themselves more self-righteous than you, which may include some in your own household!

Do you think I came to bring peace on earth? No, I tell you, but division. From now on there will be five in one family divided against each other, three against two and two against three. They will be divided, father against son and son against father, mother against daughter and daughter against mother, mother-in-law against daughter-in-law and daughter-in-law against mother-in-law." LUKE 12:51-53

As I taught the apostles and some of the disciples more *difficult* things, which My Father in Heaven instructed Me to teach, there were many who walked away!

Even after following Me for two years! They witnessed the *miracles*!

They went on *Divine Assignments* and had the power to heal, and even *break holds* which the Enemy had on men, women and children!

These who walked away…listened to the Enemy and his cohorts!

… They were NOT rooted in Truth!

… They were NOT believing in the Messiah!

… They were NOT changed in Spirit!

… They stayed only because of their curiosity!

… They laughed only because their eyes saw what was on the surface!

… They falsely reported only part of what their ears heard…and their eyes witnessed!

I, the LORD of lords…the KING of kings…came down to Earth to save…from an eternity in hell…all who would truly believe!

As they left…they laughed and shook their heads! 'Did you ever hear such '*foolishness*' from this 'so-called' Messiah?'

"I tell you the truth, whoever hears my word and believes him who sent me has eternal life and will not be condemned; he has crossed over from death to life. JOHN 5:24

This is the very reason why I need you, My dearest and most trusted friends…to be available for Divine Assignments!

After My Ascension into Heaven, many of the disciples gathered with the other sons and daughters of the KING!

Blessed are you who believe in the Son of Man…Who is the SON OF GOD!

The *mystery* of the Son of Man being both Spirit and Human…is no longer a mystery to those of you who are Born-Again!

You have *stepped over* the threshold of mere humanity and taken on the *power of the Holy Spirit*!

You can do what I did…AND MORE…IF you believe!

'LORD' you say, 'I do believe, but I still can not do all You did! Why?'

Oh, dear child! Have you learned of the Gifts of the Spirit? No one… NOT ONE…has all of the Gifts!

As I have told you in My Holy Word! To each is assigned a certain and special Gift!

Gather together!

Look around at each son or daughter!

…Who has more wisdom?

…Who has more knowledge?

…Who has more faith?

…Who has more power to heal?

…Who has more power for miracles?

…Who has more thought to prophesy?

…Who has more discernment of good and evil spirits?

…Who has more ability to speak in tongues?

…Who has more understanding to interpret these tongues?

? Are you not receiving all these Gifts
from the same HOLY SPIRIT?

Is it not up to the same HOLY SPIRIT to give the Gifts to each one…
just as He determines?

- ♥ I was grateful for whatever the Father gave Me as the Son of Man…
through the power of the HOLY SPIRIT!
- ♥ I knew I had to ask with the right intention, and with a **true and
believing heart**!
- ♥ When you pray…how is your heart?
- ♥ Remember! I Am with you as you pray!
- ♥ Is your heart as humble as a child's?

Think…meditate on these words through My Apostle, Paul:

*Be imitators of God, therefore, as dearly loved children and live a life of
love, just as Christ loved us and gave himself up for us as a fragrant offering and
sacrifice to God.* EPHESIANS 5:1-2

You see, dearest one, what I did, you can surely do!

I speak NOT of things that are done to be seen, nor to be understood
by humanity!

I speak of things, which are BEYOND HUMAN UNDERSTANDING!

I speak of the Fruits, which you can produce through the Power of the
HOLY SPIRIT, within your heart, your mind, your soul, your spirit!

*But the fruit of the Spirit is love, joy, peace, patience, kindness, goodness,
faithfulness, gentleness and self-control. Against such things there is no law.*
GALATIANS 5:22-23

Those of you who belong to ME, JESUS the Messiah, have crucified
your sinful natures! All with its passions and desires!

- ♥ Many of My beautiful, faithful and obedient disciples, who have
lived on Earth, are now with your LORD!
- ♥ They accomplished their Blessed Assignments!

Through much pain and suffering…spiritually, mentally, emotionally
and physically!

- ♥ Some planted seeds!
- ♥ Others watered these spiritual seeds!
- ♥ Others have gathered the Harvest…for the Almighty One!

Whatever they have done…YOU CAN, as well!
Come! I will give all you need!
Come! I will fill you with JOY!
Come! I will anoint and bless you…for all Divine Assignments!
**I AM HE…WHO LOVES AND FORGIVES
YOU…BEYOND MEASURE!**

I Am Christ the KING!
I Am your Beloved Savior,
  Jesus

! DO YOU PRAY THROUGH MY HOLY SPIRIT? !

I will give them an undivided heart and put a new spirit in them;
I will remove from them their heart of stone and give them a heart
of flesh. Then they will follow my decrees and be careful to keep
my laws. They will be my people, and I will be their God.
EZEKIEL 11:19-20

God is spirit, and his worshipers must worship in spirit and in truth."
JOHN 4:24

O' My Dearest Disciple,

The Father is pleased with the *sensitivity* of My friends!

This *sensitivity* can only come from *searching* for the *power* of the HOLY SPIRIT…to *pray* according to the FATHER's Perfect Will!

My time on Earth was blessed with Joy…when I was able to have time to visit with 'little ones'…the infants, the babies, the little boys and girls who were approaching the 'age of reason'!

Do you wonder, as to *why* a baby, or young child… may look up to the sky, or towards the ceiling…and nothing is apparent to you…and they just stare…their eyes opened wide and a sweet smile on their faces?

♥ I share with you now…that baby…or child…is seeing activity in the *heavenly dimension*!

♥ That little one is seeing their Guardian Angel…and their Angel who sits before the feet of the Father!

♥ This is because of their *complete purity* and *innocence*!

Many parents are twice blessed to give birth to a child…AND that child does not mature normally…however, stays as innocent as the day they were born!

They grow older, yet their mind, spirit, soul, and heart **remain** as little—precious—children…**innocent forever**!

Therefore, the Enemy prowls around the Earth, to try and rob them of their *innocence*…through adults…who have *evil* in their hearts and minds!

"Whoever welcomes one of these little children in my name welcomes me; and whoever welcomes me does not welcome me but the one who sent me."
MARK 9:37

I had appointed seventy-two disciples…sending them out—two by two—to go out and bring in a *harvest of souls!*

When they returned…still in such wonderment at the power I had bestowed on them…they were filled with **joy** that even the demons *submitted* to them in My Name!

He replied, "I saw Satan fall like lightening from heaven. I have given you authority to trample on snakes and scorpions and to overcome all the power of the enemy; nothing will harm you.

However, do not rejoice that the spirits submit to you, but rejoice that your names are written in heaven."

At that time Jesus, full of joy through the Holy Spirit, said, "I praise you, Father, Lord of heaven and earth, because you have hidden these things from the wise and learned, and revealed them to little children. Yes, Father, for this was your good pleasure. LUKE 10:18-20

Are my disciples, in these last days, as excited as were My first apostles and disciples?

- ♥ Remember, I **gave** them the *power* of the HOLY SPIRIT! Since I had not, as yet, returned to the Father…they had **not received the infilling of the HOLY SPIRIT within each of their hearts**!
- ♥ If they were filled with such Joy, *before* receiving the HOLY SPIRIT… they had **unquenchable Joy** after they were BORN-AGAIN!
- ♥ **Without** being filled with *power* from the HOLY SPIRIT, Himself… you can **not** truly **know** the ONE TRUE GOD!
- ♥ **Without** the HOLY SPIRIT…you can **not** believe in Three Divine Persons of the Blessed Trinity:
                THE FATHER—ELOHIM!
           THE SON—YESHUA HA'MACHIACH!
                THE HOLY SPIRIT!
- ✝ ELOHIM…GOD THE CREATOR!
- ✝ YESHUA HA'MACHIACH…JESUS THE MESSIAH!
- ✝ THE SPIRIT…HOLY AND POWERFUL!

Whose *Voice* do you hear through this message?

~ ABBA's?

~ The CHRIST's?

~ The HOLY SPIRIT's?

Or, has the *cacophony* of the world…drowned out *all* our Voices?

Are you *truly* and *completely* filled with the HOLY SPIRIT?

If you are, cherished friend, then there is **not a single moment** in which you are not thinking or praying to the Father…in the Name of JESUS, the Son…and in the Power of the HOLY SPIRIT! Is this not true?

Whatever situation you are experiencing…whatever pain may be assaulting you…whatever circumstance is beyond your control…YOU, most blessed disciple, exhibit MY JOY…wherever you are…and wherever you go!!!

You are free in Me…because you allow the HOLY SPIRIT to *organize* and *orchestrate* your days…at home…at work…and anywhere in between!

Dear friends, do not believe every spirit, but test the spirits to see whether they are from God, because many false prophets have gone out into the world. This is how you can recognize the Spirit of God: Every spirit that acknowledges that Jesus Christ has come in the flesh is from God, but every spirit that does not acknowledge Jesus is not from God. This is the spirit of the antichrist, which you have heard is coming and even now is already in the world.

You, dear children, are from God and have overcome them, because the one who is in you is greater than the one who is in the world. They are from the world and therefore speak from the viewpoint of the world, and the world listens to them. We are from God, and whoever knows God listens to us; but whoever is not from God does not listen to us. This is how we recognize the Spirit of truth and the spirit of falsehood. 1 JOHN 4:1-6

Therefore, precious and faithful disciple, you must pray for *hearts to soften*…and for *minds* of men and women, and even children…*to see the evils of the day!*

† As you continue in My Divine Assignments…
    understand and beware…you are putting the Enemy and his fallen angels…into a whirlwind!

† They will do that…which I, alone, will allow!

† This is not to cause My followers to fail…but to make each of you *stronger!*

Stronger in the Spirit…with Wisdom, Knowledge, Understanding, Discernment, and Spiritual Insight!

Come unto ME…in the Name of My SON…JESUS, the Savior of the world!

Come unto ME…in the Power of the HOLY SPIRIT, the Helper and Guide!

Come unto ME…with Holy Boldness…I AM EL GIBBOR—GOD Almighty!

When it is time, I will 'move Heaven and Earth', and give the word to blow the Trumpet, for My Son to come and take you from the Earth…the

dead in Christ first, then those who are still alive will meet Him in the air…
all in the Blink of an eye!

Ask Me anything…in the Name of My SON—JESUS!

YOU…TREASURED DISCIPLE…
ARE LOVED BEYOND MEASURE!

I AM WHO AM,
   ABBA,
    Y H W H

! MY PLANS COME FIRST !

"This, then, is how you should pray:
" 'Our Father in heaven,
hallowed be your name,
your kingdom come,
your will be done
on earth as it is in heaven.
Give us today our daily bread.
Forgive us our debts,
as we also have forgiven our debtors.
And lead us not into temptation,
but deliver us from the evil one.'
MATTHEW 6:9-13

O' My Dearest Disciples,

† Have you not HEARD?

† Have you not KNOWN?

† Have you not LISTENED?

Do you wonder as to why your LORD allows each disciple to experience many things in the human sense and, especially, in the spiritual realm? There is much to learn in the spiritual realm! With your human mind, this is difficult to understand! In Heaven…there is no such difficulty!

!WE KNOW … BECAUSE WE KNOW!

Do you realize you are being taught now…on Earth…for what you will be called to do in Eternity? You *must* grasp this, dear friend! This is another one of the Kingdom secrets, that I have shared with you! With you…those I call My friends…My companions!

The *spiritual* is the most important! Your minds, your hearts, your souls, must always be on your LORD…*listening* for My voice…*closing* your ears to the cacophony of the human world! Remember…I have told you… you can do this if you are alone, or you can do this if you are in a crowd!

When you hear My voice…look up! Close your ears to the sounds of those in the world!

♥ I will give you secrets of Heaven, that I offer no one else!

♥ I will give you the Keys to the Kingdom!

Imagine this, dear one! **The Keys to the Kingdom of Heaven**…only a few are able to have! And they are not on *loan*…they are for you to **own**, that

74

you may come into the Kingdom...before the Throne...and speak to ABBA and to Me, as I sit at His right hand!

Your mind will be blessed, if you think clearly of grasping the truth of Heaven and Earth!

Our relationship cannot be an *emotional* one...it must be of Spirit and Truth! This is why I am the Rock! The Rock stands strong! *Human emotions* do not!

"But, LORD", you say! "What of *love?*"

What of love, dear one? It is to be *unconditional*...like a *rock*...strong and steadfast!

Your *heart* is what guides the *unconditional love*, which connects to your *mind*...and all the **evil** and all the **good** comes from the **heart through the mind**!

!Understand this!

Since, then, you have been raised with Christ, set your hearts on things above, where Christ is seated at the right hand of God. Set your minds on things above, not on earthly things. For you died, and your life is now hidden with Christ in God. COLOSSIANS 3:1-3

There are those of you who have been given Kingdom Assignments... Special Commissions...that were placed in you, before you were born!

♥ You were *born* with a purpose!
♥ You must *live* for this purpose!
♥ The *ultimate purpose* is to bring GLORY, PRAISE, WORSHIP and ADORATION to the FATHER!

!Understand this also!

Those of My disciples whose bodies are not as strong as others...who are weak with illnesses...who have been prayed for, and are still being prayed for...yet, the conditions remain; and you say that God has *not heard* your prayers...

GOD ALWAYS HEARS YOUR PRAYERS!

God always sees the love in your hearts for those for whom you pray! However, **God's plans come first**!

Many healings are allowed to come quickly, because that illness or that condition is not part of the person's commission for your LORD! Those who remain in their illnesses, or in their conditions have a commission to fulfill...*because of those conditions*!

Do you hear Me not, dear disciple? Open your ears to your hearts and understand!

A child falls and cuts his knee and you pray, "LORD...heal my child's knee!" That knee is healed, because it is not part of the *child's mission* on earth! It is **your** part!

You show the *faith* and the *obedience* and the *trust* through your prayers for your child!

Everything has a purpose in the Kingdom of Heaven!

And we know that in all things God works for the good of those who love him, who have been called according to his purpose. ROMANS 8:28

* There are many that suffer from critical illnesses!
* There are many that are disabled, blind, mute, deaf!
* There are many whose minds remain as a child, although they are physically adults!
* There are those who are suffering from starvation, from beatings, from torture, from abandonment, from molestation!

My people should love them and pray for them! That is every true disciple's commission!

It is the Father's *will* if He will heal! However, **He always hears**!

There are many things you must accept while on this Earth! This Earth belongs to Satan! He causes much turmoil! And…yes…the Father CAN stop him…however, He sometimes waits to see what His people will do first!

Remember Paul! He accepted the *thorns in the flesh*! Do you think that the other apostles and disciples did not pray for him? THEY DID… EARNESTLY! However, they had to learn to PRAISE Me for Paul's *thorns and pain*…as he did!

✝ PRAISE Me for the illnesses and diseases that continue!
✝ PRAISE Me for those who are have suffered mentally, and physically…and still do!

As you read or hear these words…there are men, women and children suffering and dying all over the Earth!

✝ PRAISE Me!
✝ WORSHIP Me!

You do not know all of the Father's plans for each person that has ever been born or will be born!

For those God foreknew he also predestined to be conformed to the likeness of his Son, that he might be the firstborn among many brothers. ROMANS 8:29

Many times, some disciples tell those prayed for, that they were *not* healed due to a lack of faith!

INTERCESSORY PRAYER is not a *contest of wills*!

The answers are ultimately GOD Almighty's alone!

His Will counts!
His Will is always Perfect!
DO NOT lose heart...nor allow those being prayed for to lose heart...for they become too discouraged...and the Enemy finds his opportunity to swoop in like a vulture!!

Be forewarned!

You must help each one to find JOY in their pain! Whatever that may be! Whether it is emotional or physical!

* All of you...all My disciples...must pray for *discernment of how to pray!*
* My disciples must listen for the promptings of the Holy Spirit...*to know what to pray!*
* My disciples must learn *spiritual insight*...for the Father's *perfect will* for each of you!

!DO NOT HAMPER THE FATHER'S PLANS!

♥ You are My blessed disciple!
♥ You are being prepared to be My Bride!

I tell you these things, not to admonish you, but to learn to *grow in the Spirit*...because ultimately...YOU WILL BE SPIRIT!

Come! Sit near Me!

Come! Let us pray together!

Come! Rest your head upon My shoulder! Feel the peace and the JOY that fills you!

Come! Take a sip from My Living Waters!

My Beloved...I AM WHO AM...
Loves You Who Are Mine...
BEYOND MEASURE!

Always remember...I will never leave you nor forsake you!

Your Master and Lover,
  Yeshua ha'Machiach

Precious Sweet-one:

The LORD foils the plans of the nations; he
thwarts the purposes of the peoples.
But the plans of the LORD stand firm forever;
the purposes of his heart through all generations.
PSALM 33:10-11

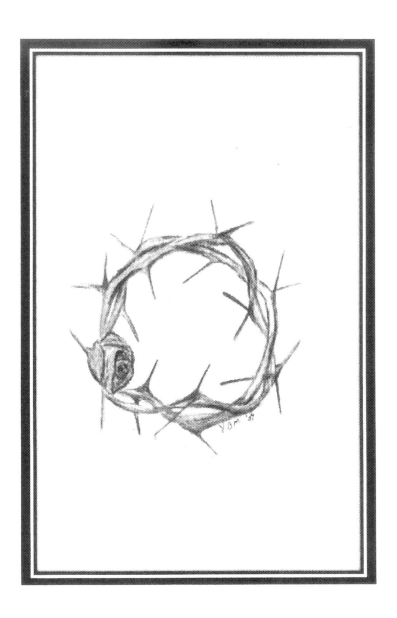

! FORGET TO FORGIVE? !

Remember, O LORD, your great mercy and love, for they are from of old.
PSALM 25:6

For the sake of your name, O LORD,
forgive my iniquity, though it is great.
Who, then, is the man that fears the LORD?
He will instruct him in the way chosen for him.
PSALM 25:11-12

For as high as the heavens are above the earth,
so great is his love for those who fear him;
as far as the east is from the west,
so far has he removed our transgressions from us.
PSALM 103:11-12

O' My Dearest Friend, My Faithful Disciple,

- ♥ Your LORD comes to you...as *often* as you invite Me!
- ♥ As *often* as you *desire* to hear My voice *beating* in your heart!
- ♥ As *often* as you set your mind on things from above!
- ♥ You, dear friend, who are reading or hearing these words yearn to have Me, your LORD, fellowship with you...*quite often*!

Is this not true?

There are times I send someone in My place! Have you discerned this encounter *often*?

Your spiritual sensitivity must stay sharp! You must have a very keen sense, so you do NOT give away the Secrets of Heaven, which I have and continue to teach you!

I must enlighten you, so that you can enlighten and love each other, as brothers and sisters!

Do not forget to entertain strangers, for by so doing some people have entertained angels without knowing it. HEBREWS 13:2

Do you truly believe, dear one, that there were times when you have also *entertained* your Blessed LORD?

Is this too difficult to imagine?

- † If YOU are able to BELIEVE in the RISEN CHRIST—
- † If YOU are able to BELIEVE in the FREE GIFT of SALVATION—

† If YOU are able to BELIEVE in the POWER OF MY GRACE—

† If YOU are able to BELIEVE in MY IMMINENT RETURN… TO TAKE YOU TO YOUR ETERNAL HOME—

Then…My dearest friend…it should **NOT** be difficult to believe your LORD of lords…your KING of kings **has spent time in your presence**!

If the Father…our ABBA…sends…and has sent…His angels…from Heaven to Earth…for your sake…it is because of His LOVE for you! It is because of this LOVE…that I find JOY in standing next to you during sad times…AND…during happy times!

I tell you these things…because your citizenship is in Heaven!

You now belong to ME! From the first moment you sought FORGIVENESS for your sins…and *asked ME* to be the **LORD of your life**…I have been as close to you as each heartbeat!

I AM your Blessed Savior!

As I have FORGIVEN YOU…you must not forget to FORGIVE anything you have against a brother or a sister!

Are you holding your brothers and sisters up in prayer?

† Many are suffering persecution for their faith in ME!

† Many are experiencing hunger, fatigue, loneliness and grief!

ALL these bring sorrow to your LORD!

Too many, who say they follow the Christ, *complain* in their health and abundance!

ALL this brings the Body of Believers into confusion, and into the path of the Enemy!

If your spiritual, emotional, physical and financial goal is to bring Glory to the Name of the Father…then you will live as a **true** man or woman of the One True Living GOD!

You will strive to be as *faithful* and *obedient* as all those who have lived before you!

You will live and bring others to your LORD…by example…NOT…by shouting your opinions or convictions of man-made religiosities!

♥ The LOVE you have for your LORD…will shine on your face!

♥ The FAITH you have in your LORD…will show in your actions!

♥ The JOY you have because of your LORD…will light up your eyes!

…Many will resent you!

…Many will be jealous of you!

…Many will turn away from you!

† The reasons are spiritual, My friend! Never human!†

For this very reason, make every effort to add to your faith goodness;

to goodness, knowledge; and to knowledge, self-control; and to self-control, perseverance; and to perseverance, godliness; and to godliness, brotherly kindness; and to brotherly kindness, love. For if you possess these qualities in increasing measure, they will keep you from being ineffective and unproductive in your knowledge of our Lord Jesus Christ. But if anyone does not have them, he is nearsighted and blind, and has forgotten that he has been cleansed from his past sins. 2 PETER 1:5-9

Have you read Peter's words carefully? Have you understood?

It is *amazing*, is it not, how Peter…a gruff fisherman…was chosen by ME to be the Rock upon whom I would build My Church?

Simon Peter addressed his two letters: 'Grace and peace be yours in abundance…'

In another letter he refers to himself as: 'a servant and apostle of Jesus Christ,' and further wrote:

To those who through the righteousness of our God and Savior Jesus Christ have received a faith as precious as ours:

Grace and peace be yours in abundance through the knowledge of God and of Jesus our Lord. 2 PETER 1-2

'A FAITH AS PRECIOUS AS OURS'!

† Peter…who wept after he had denied Me three times, just as I had foretold!

† Peter…who understood My forgiveness, and believed I promised to forget!

† Peter…who had so much love for his LORD, felt it a dishonor to be crucified as his LORD was, and therefore requested to be crucified upside down!

Such *honor*…such *respect*…such *sacrifice*…he gave to his LORD!

And you, dear friend? Are there those who still await *your* forgiveness?

Or perhaps, you have forgiven; however, mention the situation whenever the desire strikes you…that you have NOT followed the **true example** of your LORD…and have tried to *forget*?

Pray for this, dear one, by asking for 'healing of memories'!

This will help you *put* and *keep* these memories…in the past…always!

You are more than a conqueror, through ME, Who loves you!

Come! Envision Me next to you!

Come! Envision My arms embracing you!

Come! Envision My love permeate every fiber of your being!

♥ SHOUT WITH JOY!

♥ SING WITH PRAISES ON YOUR LIPS!
**I AM HE…WHO LOVES YOU
BEYOND MEASURE!**

Your Divine Friend,
Jesus

! I HAVE LIFTED YOU HIGHER !

But those who wait on the LORD
Shall renew their strength;
They shall mount up with wings like eagles,
They shall run and not be weary,
They shall walk and not faint.
ISAIAH 40:31 NKJV

O' My Dearest Friends…My Faithful Disciples,

Our ABBA is filled with JOY while watching how My friends HONOR, WORSHIP, PRAISE and GLORIFY Me to others!

I know your hearts! I know what is in your minds! Continue to pray for discernment and spiritual insight! The things you will experience, because of your love for Me, are not available to every one!

…Do you not feel it?

…Do you not understand it?

…Have you not hoped for it?

…Have you not looked for it?

I have lifted you up higher and higher toward the heavens! You can *see* and *feel* another dimension! This is reserved only for My faithful and obedient disciples who are truly My friends!

There is so much ugliness in the world today! So much hate! So much destruction! So much greed! So much idol worship! This is why I need you to be *faithful* and *obedient* to My Voice!

- ♥ I need you to pray unceasingly for the **children** of this world!
- ♥ I need you to pray for the **elderly people,** who cannot help themselves!
- ♥ I need you to pray for those who are **suffering, because of their faith in Me**!
- ♥ I need you to pray for those who have so much hatred in their hearts for another **race** or **creed**!

Continue earnestly in prayer, being vigilant in it with thanksgiving;
COLOSSIANS 4:2 NKJV

You, My friends, have been coming closer to Me, and desire for My return! I cannot tell you how much JOY this gives Me!

I do not know when I will return…only the Father knows! However, there is much for you to do during this time!

Do not forget to look up and keep your eyes on your LORD!

Your Savior weeps, watching ABBA's creation, being cruel to those who are weaker and destitute!

You must wonder, why I speak of JOY, and then I speak of sadness, of how ABBA's creation saddens your LORD! It has been like this from the beginning!

However, My friends, My disciples, know that I will never leave you nor forsake you!

You may be experiencing terrible times in your lives! Perhaps illness! Perhaps financial needs! Perhaps the loss of loved ones! Be not afraid! All these things are *temporary*!

- ✝ Stand strong!
- ✝ Remember the Cross!
- ✝ Remember…there is no Valley of the Shadow of Death for you!
- ✝ Trust only in Me, your Savior, your LORD, your Messiah…the One Who *loves you beyond measure*!
- ✝ Stay close to Me, dearest! If I allow you to have visions…it is because I love you! It is because I desire to encourage you! It is because you have opened your heart to Me…the LORD of lords, the KING of kings!

This is why you must pray, fervently, for those **who have hardened their hearts against Me**!

They are *afraid* to believe! They cannot let go of the world's enticements… and be free in Me…just as you are!

- ♥ Do you not feel free, My precious one? Yes, you do!
- ♥ You are free, indeed, because you have given yourself to Me!
- ♥ You belong to Me, now! Every part of you is filled with My Spirit! The Truth will be shown at the right time!

Those who do not believe, will be scattered and in terrible agony! Those who would want to believe, will have the opportunity to open their hearts, for the last time, before My return!

Remember, your loved ones are sanctified through you! I know the desire you have for them…it is the same desire that I have…for no one to be left behind!

For the unbelieving husband is sanctified by the wife, and the unbelieving wife is sanctified by the husband; otherwise your children would be unclean, but now they are holy. 1 CORINTHIANS 7:14 NKJV

Continue to PRAISE Me for the day that they finally open their eyes and see the Truth! Will that not be glorious, dear ones?

Now come! Rest with Me!

Come! Sit here next to Me! Place your head on My Shoulder!

...Feel My PEACE!

...Feel My JOY come through to you!

Come! Look unto Heaven...the time is short...and you will be coming Home soon!

ABBA, Yeshua, and the Holy Spirit...
Love You Above And Beyond
The Measure of Eternity!

♥ You are Mine!

♥ You are My Beloved!

I am your KING!

I AM Who AM,

Jesus

! TOO SPIRITUALLY AMBITIOUS? !

For when I preach the gospel, I cannot boast, since I am
compelled to preach. Woe to me if I do not preach the gospel!
1 CORINTHIANS 9:16

We do not want you to be uninformed, brothers, about the hardships we
suffered in the province of Asia. We were under great pressure, far beyond our
ability to endure, so that we despaired even of life. Indeed, in our hearts we felt
the sentence of death. But this happened that we might not rely on ourselves
but on God, who raises the dead. He has delivered us from such a deadly peril,
and he will deliver us. On him we have set our hope that he will continue to
deliver us, as you help us by your prayers. Then many will give thanks on our
behalf for the gracious favor granted us in answer to the prayers of many.
2 CORINTHIANS 1:8-11

O' My Dearest and Precious Children,

How are you using your *spiritual wisdom…*your *anointed discernment…*
your *blessed understanding…*your *scriptural knowledge?*

The Father does not desire to use you, as if you were a 'broom', sweeping
evil under a rug! Sooner or later, the 'rug' will have to be lifted and thoroughly
cleaned!

   *   What the *Father* desires…

     *   What the *Son* needs…

       *   What the *Holy Spirit* accomplishes…

…is for Our disciples to use the **spiritual talents**, the **spiritual gifts,**
along with **worldly treasures**—earned from honest work—and **earthly
time**…*for* Our Glory!

Worldly ambitions do not consider spiritual ambitions…nor can they
be compared to Heaven's Glory!

Whatever you do…wherever you go…there should be

… One thing that should consume your *heart's* desire!

… One thing which should occupy your *mind* and your *spirit!*

That *one thing*, dear disciple, is **how to bring Honor and Glory to your
LORD and KING—your MESSIAH!**

  ♥   You, dear one, must *live* and *love* to serve others, in order to bring
them into fellowship with Christ!

♥ You, precious disciple, must *yearn* with all that is within you, to bring GLORY to your Savior!

♥ You, cherished heart, must *desire*, above all else to teach others how to Magnify GOD Almighty's SON, Who suffered, died and rose again to bring Salvation to mankind!

♥ You, blessed disciple, must *labor*, with all that is within you, to *honor* and *follow* the guidance of the Holy Spirit!

Can you be too ambitious **in** and **for** GOD's desires...**His will to be done on Earth as it is in Heaven?**

Are you feeling *compelled*, dear one, to spread the Good News for CHRIST's sake?

Being obedient and faithful to the Father and the Son and the Holy Spirit...willingly and completely...will bring blessings which are above and beyond what you could ever hope for in this world!

Not blessings which those who live for worldly ambitions desire... which are here today and gone tomorrow...but the blessings which are for *your Eternal Glory!*

Praise to the God and Father of our Lord Jesus Christ, the Father of compassion and the God of all comfort, who comforts us in all our troubles, so that we can comfort those in any trouble with the comfort we ourselves have received from God. 2 CORINTHIANS 1:3-5

Does not Paul speak of such blessings which the world sees as having no value?

How much is 'comfort' worth...to someone who has never needed it?

How much is 'compassion' worth...to someone who can not understand it?

Should a disciple of the LORD of lords not pursue such *ambition?*

The *ambition* to know when to give comfort?

The *ambition* to understand when true compassion

...honest and sincere...is to be displayed?

† Does not EL GIBBOR—GOD ALMIGHTY—have this very ambition, dear disciple?

† Does not JEHOVAH-shalom—have the 'holy ambition' to *bring* to you, and *leave* unto you—His Blessed Peace?

† Does not JEHOVAH-nissi—have this same 'holy ambition' to grant you Victory over the evil one, Satan?

What kind of *ambition* have **you**, chosen disciple, been called to accomplish by the Master—your ADONAI?

Are you trying to win the approval of human beings...or of GOD?

Are you trying to please people...or GOD, Himself?

I tell you, dearest heart, you read the Scriptures and messages written through inspiration of the HOLY SPIRIT, in order to gain wisdom and true understanding of what the LORD GOD desires from you!

`If you were trying to please people, or, win approval of mere human beings, then you would not be serving Christ Jesus!

- ♥ It is He Who *speaks* to you now!
- ♥ It is He Who *loves* you forever!
- ♥ It is He Who *died willingly* from 'holy ambition' to save your soul from an eternity in the pit of hell!

Remember these things—which are TRUTHS spoken by the KING of kings...through the power of the HOLY SPIRIT!

When you decide what you will do on the morrow...without *seeking My perfect will first*...how does your day go?

...smoothly?

...peacefully?

...joyfully?

Think who you were trying to please... others?...yourself?

Did you remember, upon arising, to *thank* Almighty GOD, first?

Did you remember, after you awoke, to *seek* the wisdom and guidance from the Holy Spirit?

The Holy Spirit desires to 'organize' and 'orchestrate' your day!

I know you wonder 'why'! Do you not, dear one?

The answer should be obvious...

People try to dictate what My disciples should or should not be doing within the church body!

If these people are not *Spirit-filled*...their suggestions will bring confusion!

Confusion to the heart and mind of My followers changes the plans I have for them!

Others may think they have 'your best interests at heart'...but they do not!

Could you have too much *spiritual ambition*...when that ambition is to win souls for the Kingdom of Heaven?

When a disciple seeks after righteousness to the Glory of GOD...there is not too much spiritual ambition!

..., because those who are led by the Spirit of God are sons of God. For you did not receive a spirit that makes you a slave again to fear, but you received the Spirit of sonship. And by him we cry Abba, Father." The Spirit himself testifies

with our spirit that we are God's children. Now if we are children, then we are heirs—heirs of God and co-heirs with Christ, if indeed we share in his sufferings in order that we may also share in his glory. ROMANS 8:14-17

These are part of Paul's words to Jews and Gentiles who were within hearing of this!

My words, through any of My True, Faithful, Obedient, and Born-again disciples, are *worthy* of spiritual ambition and **Life Everlasting**!

- ♥ Boast of your relationship to ME!
  - ♥ Boast of your reliance on ME!
    - ♥ Boast of your love for ME!
- ♥ Boast only of what your LORD does for you!
  - ♥ Boast **not** of what you do out of selfish accomplishments…but…
    - ♥ Boast of My Spiritual Ambitions!

GO! My friend!

GO! My blessed one!

GO! My dearest one!

Bring My JOY…

    My LOVE…

        My MESSAGE…into all the world!

            I LOVE YOU BEYOND MEASURE!

        Awaiting Your Day In Glory,

Your KING,

    Jesus

! HOW CAN YOU
ENDURE TODAY? !

You also be patient. Establish your hearts,
for the coming of the Lord is at hand.
JAMES 5:8

For consider Him who endured such hostility from sinners against
Himself, lest you become weary and discouraged in your souls.
HEBREWS 12:3 NKJV

O' My Dearly Loved Disciple,

Be assured, dearest disciple, that I speak to you now, as you are reading or hearing this message…at exactly the perfect time in your life!

How are Our people, Our precious followers, *enduring* in these last days?

Are you waiting *anxiously* for My return?

Are you using this time, *wisely*?

It is to your *spiritual advantage* that you keep doing the work of the LORD, your GOD…

…assisting all those in need of temporal, as well as, spiritual needs!

…teaching others through wise decisions and humble actions!

…speaking of personal testimonies wherever the circumstance is similar to yours…and only through the prompting of the Holy Spirit!

- ♥ **comfort** others, as I have comforted you!
- ♥ **bless** others, as I have blessed you!
- ♥ **anoint** others, as I have anointed you!
- ♥ **pray** for others, as I have and still continue to pray for you!
- ♥ **forgive** others, as I have forgiven you!
- ♥ **accept** others, as I have accepted you!
- ♥ **love** others, as I have, and continue, to love you!

Love suffers long and is kind; love does not envy; love does not parade itself, is not puffed up; does not behave rudely, does not seek its own, is not provoked, thinks no evil; does not rejoice in iniquity, but rejoices in the truth; bears all things, believes all things, hopes all things, endures all things. Love never fails. 1 CORINTHIANS 13:4-8 NKJV

Will these things be too difficult for you, dear disciple?

I can do all things through Christ who strengthens me. PHILIPPIANS 4:13 NKJV

Paul wrote through inspiration of the HOLY SPIRIT!

Why, dear disciple? Was he, as all of Our disciples should be, not *consumed and compelled* to preach Christ crucified?

Was he not in My Presence on the road to Damascus?

Therefore, if you truly believe the complete transformations in all of Our chosen disciples, other than Judas Iscariot, then, you believe their tenacity...they never were able to deny their faith in the LORD Jesus... even suffering tortures, and imprisonments, and the penalty of death in horrid ways!

What of your own experiences, dear disciple?

Are you living, even enduring, a myriad of difficulties...spiritual, emotional, physical and financial...because you, yourself, **believe without a doubt**...that you will be risen with Christ Jesus on the last day?

A true disciple of the CHRIST...can **not** pretend enduring for the promise of the Resurrection!

"Not everyone who says to Me, 'Lord, Lord', shall enter the kingdom of heaven, but he who does the will of My Father in heaven. MATTHEW 7:21 NKJV

Though you have not seen ME...yet you still continue to believe in ME!

There are those of you, reading or hearing these words...who are undergoing tremendous trials, at this very moment in time!

† How do you *endure* the pain you suffer in your body...which never seems to decrease?

† How do you *endure* emotional upheavals...which seem to 'rain' down on your life continuously?

† How do you *endure* financial crises...that occur constantly?

† How do you *endure* the loss of family and friends...which is happening too rapidly?

Are those who do not have to endure any of these things...more at *peace* with themselves and others?

Are those who live to attain riches and fame...more *joyful* in their own existence?

Is it not true...that those who are rich...get richer...and those who are poor...become poorer?

Am I not the GOD of the rich and the poor?

Many of the rich do not even think about the existence of Almighty GOD!

Yet, the poor are always at My feet…seeking for daily sustenance!

Yet, the poor are more generous to others…than most of the rich!

However, dear disciple, the rich must *endure* things, which the poor do not!

A rich man must always *wonder* if his friends are true to him for his friendship alone, and not for his money or fame!

A rich man must endure family members who *pretend* to love him for him, and not for his money!

Now, what of the poor man?

He endures love and respect for himself alone, not for what he can give…for he has nothing…except something which is more difficult to attain than riches and fame…an *honorable reputation*!

A good name is to be chosen rather than great riches,
Loving favor rather than silver and gold. PROVERBS 22:1 NKJV

Therefore, dearest disciple, how do you achieve a *good name*?

Is it more *important* for you to prove yourself to man…or to GOD?

Who is it that holds your *spirit* and *soul* in His Hand…Man or GOD?

It is neither…until **you decide** whom to follow…as you *endure* in your life's daily struggles!

Only by permission of the Almighty One…Satan, Our Enemy, can and will make your life quite difficult!

Because of his evil tactics…too many men and women, fall into utter despair, and deny the One Who holds the future in His Mighty Hands!

Therefore, blessed disciple, being *righteous* and *just* to all people… without prejudice…will gain for yourself a *good name*!

However, how do you become a *righteous* and *just* person?

Not by following Satan's schemes…but…by following the *example* I, the Messiah, set before you while on the Earth!

✝ Doing what is *right* in the eyes of GOD!

✝ Seeking *justice* for every one!

✝ Being *not afraid* to speak the truth with Holy Boldness!

‼ FOLLOWING GOD'S BLESSED
AND PERFECT WILL ‼

Many will hate you for being *righteous* and *just*…if it interferes with their own evil plans!

How will you *endure* the evil actions...which will be thrust upon you in many ways?

Are you able to leave the future in the hands of the LORD of lords?

You must be patient...until the time of My return...which is not long from now...only the Father knows the day and the hour!

Your hearts must be ready...and will be...as you *endure* these last days!

Do not grumble against one another, brethren, lest you be condemned. Behold, the Judge is standing at the door!

My brethren, take the prophets, who spoke in the name of the Lord, as an example of suffering and patience.

Indeed we count them blessed who endure. You have heard of the perseverance of Job and seen the end intended by the Lord—that the Lord is very compassionate and merciful. JAMES 5:9-11 NKJV

- ♥ Have you *understood*, dear one?
- ♥ Have you *listened* with your heart?
- ♥ Have you *endured* all for My sake?
- ♥ Have you *felt* My love surround you?
- ♥ Have you *desired* to be in the Presence of the KING of kings, O' beloved disciple?

Am I NOT with you *wherever* you go...*wherever* you may be at any moment?

Then you know JEHOVAH-shammah!

As a true and faithful and obedient disciple...filled to overflowing with the JOY and PEACE of the LORD...through the power of the HOLY SPIRIT...nothing can come between us!

Come to ME, in your days of trouble!

Come to ME, in your times of weakness!

Come to ME, in your moments of temptations!

With your Beloved Redeemer...there is nothing you can not *endure*!

My arms are always open to receive you...just as you are!

Dearly cherished disciple...
I, the LORD of lords...the KING of kings...
LOVE YOU BEYOND THE MEASURE
OF YOUR ENDURANCE!

The Savior of the World,
Jesus

! ARE YOU MY BELOVED? !

*This is the blessing that Moses the man of God pronounced on
the Israelites before his death. About Benjamin he said: "Let the
beloved of the LORD rest secure in him, for he shields him all day
long, and the one the LORD loves rests between his shoulders."*
DEUTERONOMY 33:1,12

*He who belongs to God hears what God says. The reason
you do not hear is that you do not belong to God."*
JOHN 8:47

*Through him and for his name's sake, we received grace and apostleship to
call people from among all the Gentiles to the obedience that comes from faith.
And you also are among those who are called to belong to Jesus Christ.*
ROMANS 1:5-6

O' My Cherished Disciple,

You…reading or hearing these words…have been *chosen* to be among
the Beloved of the Most High GOD…the One…the Only…the Almighty
Creator of all!

ABBA takes much delight in seeing how each disciple lives to be closer
to His One and Only Begotten Son—JESUS, the Messiah!

I desire to reveal many 'secrets' of the Kingdom of Heaven!

My first followers were in awe as they listened to Me speak, daily, to the
crowds which came to us each day!

Though I spoke in Parables…the men and women, and even the
children, hung on to every word I uttered!

Why, do *you* dear disciple, *think* that it was as I have said?

- ♥ *Visualize*, for a moment, that you are sitting next to Me…surrounded
  by the apostles and disciples…looking at all the faces in the crowd…
  young and old, alike!
- ♥ *Listen*, to the whispers of the children…babies crying softly…goats,
  lambs, sheep, cows…even dogs and cats and birds flying over us…
  all making such diverse sounds, as I spoke!
- ♥ *Look*, at each face…in rapt attention to the words of the Rabbi…
  Who *teaches with an authority* never before seen in all of Galilee…
  nor anywhere else!

Even the Pharisees, the Chief Priests, the Sanhedrin and the Sadducees…must marvel at My messages…My teachings…including the *sound* of My Voice!

The disciples felt a certain *pride* at being followers of Some One Who constantly stunned the Jews, who asked questions, in order to *trap* their Adonai—their Master!

Many times, thinking I had not heard them whispering among themselves, they kept wondering: 'Who IS this MAN?

'We saw Him change *water* into *wine*…right before us!'

'That is not as amazing as when He *healed* those two men from Leprosy; and gave *sight* to the man *born blind*!'

'What of raising that child who was *dead*?'

'How did He feed five thousand…with a *few pieces* of fish and bread? What kind of Power does He have?'

Then, even quieter voices would say to the others, 'He said **we** would be able to do **all** those things—AND EVEN MORE! If we **truly believe**!'

- ✦ 'BELIEVE!!'
- ✦ 'BELIEVE WHAT?'
- ✦ 'BELIEVE HOW?!

'Yet, brothers, **why** do we *continue* to follow Him?!'

'Were you all not **stunned** when Lazarus came out of his tomb?'

'My heart was so moved, when I saw Jesus weep…I had to hide my face…so no one would see me cry, as well,' one said!

Jesus wept. JOHN 11:35

O dear and treasured soul! Have you not discussed these very thoughts with other believers?

Yes, these questions and even more!

However, have you *weighed* the questions…by *searching* for the *answers* in My Holy Scriptures?

?How do you *know*, for sure, that *you belong to GOD?*

- † GOD…Who Is Omnipotent!
- † GOD…Who Is Omnipresent!
- † GOD…Who Is Omniscient!

? How do you **know**, for sure, and **Whom** has **revealed** the **Truth to you**?

Anyone can *say* Who JESUS of Nazareth *could be*…and *believe* all the *historical accounts* of My existence!

However, the question, will *still remain*, as to **My True Divinity**!

Does this question still not puzzle humanity?

When Jesus came to the region of Caesarea Philippi, he asked his disciples, "Who do people say the Son of Man is?"

They replied, "Some say John the Baptist; others Elijah; and still others, Jeremiah or one of the prophets."

"But what about you?" he asked. "Who do you say I am?"

Simon Peter answered, "You are the Christ, the Son of the living God."

Jesus replied, "Blessed are you, Simon son of Jonah, for this was not revealed to you by man, but by my Father in heaven. And I tell you that you are Peter, and on this rock I will build my church, and the gates of Hades will not overcome it. I will give you the keys of the kingdom of heaven; whatever you bind on earth will be bound in heaven, and whatever you loose on earth will be loosed in heaven." Then he warned his disciples not to tell anyone he was the Christ. MATTHEW 16:13-20

Therefore, you, reading or hearing these words…have also been given the Key of Heaven…as to the **Truth** of **Who** the Son of Man is…and **Why** and **How** I…JESUS of Nazareth…**AM** the **SON OF THE LIVING GOD**!!!

The Father gave the revelation to Peter!

After My Death, Resurrection, and Ascension into Heaven…I sent the HOLY SPIRIT!

♥ Yes…you are My Beloved!

You did not choose me, but I chose you and appointed you to go and bear fruit—fruit that will last. Then the Father will give you whatever you ask in my name. This is my commandment: Love each other. JOHN 15:16-17

♥ Therefore, My beloved disciple, will you *desire to follow all that I command or ask of you?*

♥ Though you are *criticized* or *hated* for what you do for your LORD?

♥ Though you suffer…and become as *broken bread* and *poured out wine?*

♥♥ ARE YOU THE BELOVED OF THE MESSIAH?

♥♥ ARE YOU THE FRIEND OF THE REDEEMER?

♥♥ ARE YOU THE SANCTIFIED OF THE SAVIOR?

May the God of hope fill you with all joy and peace as you trust in him, so that you may overflow with hope by the power of the Holy Spirit. ROMANS 15:13

YOU…Cherished Disciple…And All Who Believe In The LORD of lords…the KING of kings…ARE LOVED BEYOND MEASURE… FOREVER!

I AM KING,
  Jesus

! ONLY FROM ME? !

And we know that in all things God works for the good of those
who love him, who have been called according to his purpose.
ROMANS 8:28

O' My Most Beloved Sons and Daughters of our Most High God,
Listen carefully to what I, the LORD of lords tells you!
† Many prophets have been sent to My people! They have warned
humanity of sins against ME...and each other!
† They have died...speaking to deaf ears and hardened hearts!
† They have praised Me for seeing them through the valleys of their
lives!
Is it not wonderful to be on a *MOUNTAIN TOP EXPERIENCE?*
Have you been able, as many of My dear friends have before you...to
GLORIFY and ADORE your LORD...also through the times of trudging
in the muck and mire days, weeks, months, or years?
Does this not all speak of My Grace?
Paul wrote, by *inspiration* of the Holy Spirit:
But because of his great love for us, God, who is rich in mercy, made us alive
with Christ even when we were dead in transgressions—it is by grace you have
been saved. And God raised us up with Christ and seated us with him in the
heavenly realms in Christ Jesus, in order that in the coming ages he might show
the incomparable riches of his grace, expressed in his kindness to us in Christ
Jesus. EPHESIANS 2:4-7
Therefore, dearest sons and daughters...I, your LORD of lords, your
KING of kings, will see to carry you through all and any trial that the
Father allows...to raise up for Himself a Holy People!
For it is by grace you have been saved, through faith—and this not from
yourselves, it is the gift of God—not by works, so that no one can boast.
EPHESIANS 2:8-9
Have **you** boasted because you have shown *Grace* to someone?
What or who, has held you back, from extending the same Grace as
your LORD?
Have you desired that someone extend Grace to you?
Each of My disciples must not only understand the *receiving* of Grace
but be *givers* of Grace, as well!
What of Mercy, dear ones?

Think back on your life – before you decided to walk closely with your LORD!

Just for an instant! As you have been taught not to look back! Not to the right, nor to the left…only forward!

Your mind, eyes, heart, spirit and your soul, should ALWAYS be with desire, to come Home, and be *forever* in the Presence of the LORD of lords…the KING of kings!

✝ Do you see the frequent times I extended Mercy…for the same indiscretion, the same sin?

✝ Do you remember the times when you failed to offer Mercy to family or friends? Or even a stranger?

Were these times so ridiculous, that you held onto *resentment…anger…bitterness*?

There are many which I, alone, can bring to your mind!

You have forgotten! Have you not?

Perhaps those you failed to extend a bit of Mercy to…are still hurting from your reaction?

Extend it NOW! Lose no time! Wait no more!

From this moment on, take to heart these words, which were inspired to Paul through the Holy Spirit:

Let your conversation be always full of grace, seasoned with salt, so that you may know how to answer everyone. COLOSIANS 4:6

Answering or speaking with Grace will be akin to *unconditional* love!

Others will not be hurt by you, so they will not hurt you…then it will not be necessary to give, nor to desire, Mercy from anyone!

O dearest ones! As you abide in ME…you will have My *mind*, My *love*, My *joy*, My *peace*!

Your will is to live on Earth as you would in Heaven…in **PERFECT HARMONY**!

YES! It is ABBA's Perfect Will…to have our chosen sons and daughters…to live on Earth…as they will in Heaven!

• As I **give** you *My unconditional love*…you are to extend it to others!

• As I **shower** on you *My blessings from above*…you are to share them with others!

• As I **bless** you with *My forgiveness, grace* and *mercy*…you should follow your LORD's example!

All that I have told you, is for you to Glorify the Father above!

✝ Following in the footsteps of the Christ is NOT easy on a human level…without Power from the HOLY SPIRIT!

† Following in the Way of the Savior, fills you with the heavenly desire to be obedient and faithful!

† Taking up your own cross daily…and walking…

…step by step!

…moment by moment!

…breath by breath!

~ until it is time for you to come Home!

~ until you fear NOT man…nor physical death!

~ until you raise your eyes and arms toward ME…and cry out in your desire to be brought to Me in love…NOT in anguish!

Come! Lie down and rest!

Come! Keep your mind stayed on Me!

My arms are always around you…My beloved sons and daughters… whom **I LOVE BEYOND MEASURE1**

I AM HE…WHO WILL ONE DAY COME FOR YOU!

Your Savior and LORD,
Yeshua

Precious Sweet-one:

Therefore, since we have a great high priest who has gone through the heavens, Jesus the Son of God, let us hold firmly to the faith we profess. For we do not have a high priest who is unable to sympathize with our weaknesses, but we have one who has been tempted in every way, just as we are—yet was without sin. Let us then approach the throne of grace with confidence, so that we may receive mercy and find grace to help us in our time of need.
HEBREWS 4:14-16

! WILL YOU HEAR MY TRUMPET BLOW? !

I declare to you, brothers, that flesh and blood cannot inherit the kingdom
of God, nor does the perishable inherit the imperishable. Listen, I tell you
a mystery: We will not all sleep, but we will all be changed—in a flash, in
the twinkling of an eye, at the last trumpet. For the trumpet will sound, the
dead will be raised imperishable, and we will be changed. For the perishable
must clothe itself with the imperishable, and the mortal with immortality.
When the perishable has been clothed with the imperishable, and the
mortal with immortality, then the saying that is written will come true:
"Death has been swallowed up in victory."
"Where, O death, is your victory?
Where, O death, is your sting?"
The sting of death is sin, and the power of sin is the law. But thanks
be to God! He gives us the victory through our Lord Jesus Christ.
Therefore, my dear brothers, stand firm. Let nothing move you.
Always give yourselves fully to the work of the Lord, because
you know that your labor in the Lord is not in vain.
1 CORINTHIANS 15:50-58

O' My Blessed Disciples,

✝ How have you been *waiting* for My return?

✝ Have you been *spending your time* in prayer…in PRAISES to the Father…in ADORATION of the Son…in following the GUIDANCE of the Holy Spirit?

✝ Have you *completely understood* this Scripture, which Paul wrote to the church in Corinth?

✝ Have you been *striving* to keep My Commandments?

Most people have no idea what the Holy Commandments are!

Do **YOU**?

This is not a test of your word-for-word *knowledge* of the Ten Commandments, which I gave to Moses on Mount Sinai!

However, the words, which I emblazoned on two tablets of stone, should be *embedded* in your hearts!

This is how you will be able to *know* what pleases your LORD… and to keep you from sinning!

In this way…you will *desire* to be faithful and obedient!

Also, in this way…you will be blessed witnesses unto Me…your LORD GOD!

Do you ever wonder *where* you may be, or *what* you may be doing, when I return for you and all My chosen?

Perhaps, you may be caught in sin?

Perhaps, you may be doing good works?

Remember the words which I told to My first apostles:

"So when you give to the needy, do not announce it with trumpets, as the hypocrites do in the synagogues and on the streets, to be honored by men. I tell you the truth, they have received their reward in full. But when you give to the needy, do not let your left hand know what your right hand is doing, so that your giving may be in secret. Then your Father, who sees what is done in secret, will reward you. MATTHEW 6:2-4

I also tell you, do NOT spend your most precious gift of time, thinking on these things!

Do NOT allow your mind to wander aimlessly on things, which have no value on Earth, nor in Heaven!

† These are open doors for the Enemy and his cohorts to tempt you to sin!

† These 'thoughts' will keep you from being alert to hear the Voice of your LORD!

† These 'thoughts' will keep you from being alert to hear the Trumpet blast heralding My imminent return!

You will fail to look up to see your 'Salvation which draweth nigh'!

My prophets have died in alerting My people to watch for My Coming!

Will YOU heed the words, which the Holy Spirit gave through My Prophet Jeremiah?

"Announce in Judah and proclaim in Jerusalem
and say:
'Sound the trumpet throughout the land!'
Cry aloud and say:
'Gather together!
Let us flee to the fortified cities!'
Raise the signal to go to Zion!
Flee for safety without delay!
For I am bringing disaster from the north, even
Terrible destruction." JEREMIAH 4:5-6

If you have not understood, that you have been chosen to bring the Good News to all people...then how will others listen and understand?

- ♥ Then...YOU must call on the Name of the LORD GOD...the ELOHIM...for grace and mercy!
- ♥ Then...YOU must call on the Name of the LORD of lords...the KING of kings...to open your spiritual eyes and ears!
- ♥ Then...YOU must call on the Name of the HOLY SPIRIT... to give you wisdom, knowledge and discern-ment!

You MUST remember to trust in the LORD forever, for the LORD is the **ROCK ETERNAL**!

And forget NOT, dearly beloved, you should be found shouting about **My Love and Salvation**!

Tell all whose *hearts are ready*, that **everyone** who calls on the Name of the LORD...**WILL BE SAVED**!

Now, dear ones, a word of caution from your Savior!

DO NOT BE BOASTFUL...as if these words and thoughts have come from *you*!

All you know and understand is from My Holy Spirit!

... *"God opposes the proud but gives grace to the humble."* JAMES 4:6

Humble yourselves before the Lord, and he will lift you up! JAMES 4:10

OUR MOST HIGH GOD IS TO BE
WORSHIPPED AND GLORIFIED!

- † It is because of CHRIST'S shed Blood...that you have been REDEEMED!
- † All those who accept the sacrifice of the Blood of the Lamb and become Born Again, are called the Children of God!

DO NOT become impatient to hear the Trumpet blast!

Even youths grow tired and weary, and young men stumble and fall; but those who hope in the LORD will renew their strength. They will soar on wings like eagles; they will run and not grow weary, they will walk and not be faint. ISAIAH 40:30-31

Therefore...remember always...I, the KING of kings, will teach you to wait!

Come! Take hold of the Master's Hand!

Come! Take hold of this Goblet of Living Water!

Come...dearest disciples...blessed and chosen ones!

Come...beloved disciple and friend!

!You Are Loved Beyond Measure!

I AM THE ADONAI...THE MASTER...
WHO HAS JUST SPOKEN TO YOU!

Your Anointed Messiah,
Jesus

! WHO WILL RECOGNIZE MY GLORY? !

Look, he is coming with the clouds,
and every eye will see him,
even those who pierced him;
and all the peoples of the earth will
mourn because of him.
So shall it be! Amen.
"I am the Alpha and the Omega," says the Lord God,
"who is, and who was, and who is to come, the Almighty."
REVELATION 1:7-8

O' My Most Faithful Disciples,

How many times are you able to remember when I manifested **My Presence**?

If you stop, at this very moment, and think back through your life…you will only be able to recall a few! Perhaps none?

You are wondering, 'Why do you ask, LORD? You know **all** things about me!'

Yes, dear one! I, the LORD, am Omniscient…knowing ALL THINGS!

However, YOU do NOT! Nor do most of you, remember the most Glorious and Divine Encounters, with which I, your LORD, have blessed you with during the past…even now!

Do you still question Me?

Are you still filled with AWE now…as you were at that moment?

Declare his glory among the nations, his marvelous deeds among all peoples.
PSALM 96:3

What is your answer? Could it be that you are, perhaps, embarrassed of your *intimate relationship* with the Savior?

Many of those who claim to believe in the Messiah, or the One True GOD…think it is merely a 'private' and 'personal' choice!

HEAR ME NOW! My people who *profess* Me as LORD, and *confess* their sins **and** claim to be Born Again…are being hypocrites when they *hide* ME in their 'spiritual closets'!

"Make a tree good and its fruit will be good, or make a tree bad and its fruit will be bad, for a tree is recognized by its fruit. You brood of vipers, how can you

who are evil say anything good? For out of the overflow of the heart the mouth speaks. MATTHEW 12:33-34

These people are giving in to fear, which comes only from the Enemy!

Many turn back to the 'religious' ways of their past!

WHY? Have you NOT been *witnesses* to answered prayer?

Have you NOT seen **MY GLORY** when gathering together to WORSHIP, PRAISE and ADORE ME?

WHY? After all you have experienced in your relationship with your LORD…what 'god' has enticed you to turn away?

For all the gods of the nations are idols, but the LORD made the heavens. Splendor and majesty are before him; strength and joy in his dwelling place. 1 CHRONICLES 16:26-27

✝ Have you NOT filled your heart with My overwhelming JOY, PEACE and LOVE?

✝ Have I NOT offered Living Waters to quench your Spiritual thirst?

✝ Have I NOT freely given My HOLY SPIRIT for you to gain *wisdom, discernment, knowledge* and *understanding?*

I, the LORD of lords…the KING of kings, have *freely given* to My chosen…to *freely receive!*

Oh, My dearest and obedient disciples! I tell you these things so you may recognize those among you who do NOT desire to come close to ME!

After you have prayed for those…who had a small taste of My Glory… **let go**…leave them to Me!

Continue to pray for those who are still searching!

Ask the Holy Spirit what to say or do…**without pushing** any of them further away!

Will you, dearest disciple, tell your LORD, 'who, *exactly*, you pray for?

✦ Are your prayers only for close family and friends?

✦ Are your prayers including requests from acquaintances…co-workers, fellow students, neighbors or from strangers you meet?

✦ Are your prayers becoming deeper and reaching for those who are 'out of the circle'?

How *deeply* do you pray?

Dearest disciple, did you know that MY GLORY is seen on your face?

Are you surprised by this question?

The next time you are together, with two or more disciples, and in deep prayer…take a look with your **spiritual eyes**!

Observe the face of each person!

That glow you see, is the manifestation of MY GLORY!

Remember the boldness of Moses! He desired for all to experience MY GLORY…as he asked ME for My Presence…to go with the people of Israel as they journeyed through the desert to the Promised Land!

After I, the LORD of lords…the KING of kings…said, 'Yes, I will do the very thing you ask'! I told Moses how pleased I was with him…and that I knew him by name!

Then Moses said, "Now show me your glory."

And the LORD said, "I will cause all my goodness to pass in front of you, and I will proclaim my name, the LORD, in your presence. I will have mercy on whom I will have mercy, and I will have compassion on whom I will have compassion. But," he said, "you cannot see my face, for no one may see me and live."

Then the LORD said, "There is a place near me where you may stand on a rock. When my glory passes by, I will put you in a cleft in the rock and cover you with my hand until I have passed by. Then I will remove my hand and you will see my back; but my face must not be seen." EXODUS 33:18-23

? What of YOU, dearest and most faithful and obedient friend?

♥ Have you experienced the GLORY OF THE LORD?

♥ Have you looked into the eyes of a newborn baby?

♥ Have you seen the look on a new Born-Again man or woman?

Then…YOU, blessed disciple, have had the privilege of seeing MY GLORY!

♥ Have you recognized My radiances?

What you see in the Earthly realm, is **nothing** compared to the GLORY in HEAVEN!

O most radiant of Our chosen…are *you*!

Those who do NOT believe in the Risen Christ are bewildered!

I call you CHOSEN! PRAISE the GOD of Heaven and of Earth and remember to:

Ascribe to the LORD, O families of nations, ascribe to the LORD glory and strength, ascribe to the LORD the glory due his name. Bring an offering and come before him; worship the LORD in the splendor of his holiness.

1 CHRONICLES 16:28-29

Come! Sing PRAISES to My Holy Name!

Come! WORSHIP the LORD with all of your heart!

Come! Raise your hands in joyful ADORATION!

Come! Join My Angel Choirs singing,

'HOLY, HOLY, HOLY, LORD GOD ALMIGHTY'!

GLORY IN HIS HOLY NAME…REJOICE!
HOLY IS HIS NAME!
I AM YOUR ROCK!
I AM HE WHO LIFTS YOU UP!
I AM HE WHO LOVES YOU BEYOND ETERNITY!
The **GLORY** Who Awaits You…MY BELOVED…AM THE SAVIOR of your Soul,

The KING of kings And LORD of lords!
Jesus

! TOO MUCH TALKING...
NOT ENOUGH LISTENING !

Here I am! I stand at the door and knock. If anyone hears my voice and opens the door, I will come in and eat with him, and he with me.
REVELATION 3:20

...for, "Everyone who calls on the name of the Lord will be saved." How, then, can they call on the one they have not believed in? And how can they believe in the one of whom they have not heard? And how can they hear without someone preaching to them? And how can they preach unless they are sent? As it is written, "How beautiful are the feet of those who bring good news!"
ROMANS 10:13-15

Even a fool is thought wise if he keeps silent, and discerning if he holds his tongue.
PROVERBS 17:28

But the LORD is in his holy temple; let all the earth be silent before him."
HABAKKUK 2:20

O' My Dearest Friend,

Open your *spiritual ears*...so you may hear the Voice of the LORD GOD!

If My disciples are *not listening* for daily instructions, then:

† What more can I tell you?

† What more can I ask of you?

† What more can I show you?

Perhaps, these questions are among your own?

Are you coming to Me with *impatience, frustration,* or *exhaustion?*

... "When will You *answer* me, LORD?"

... "When will You *supply* what I need?"

... "When will You *bless* the desires of my heart?"

... "When will Your *promise* come to pass?"

! BE SILENT AND LISTEN !

Now, My questions to you, dear one!

... When will you begin to *bear spiritual fruit?*

... When will you use your *spiritual gifts* to ABBA's Glory?

… When will you begin *dying to self* and *love un-conditionally?*

… When will you *surrender* your *heart, mind, spirit,* and your *soul*—completely to your SAVIOR?

The Father's timing in answering prayers **is always perfect**!

However, many of Our disciples, who *say* they are Christ-followers…do not make themselves *available* at the requests of Father GOD…nor of GOD the SON…not even at the *spiritual nudging* from the HOLY SPIRIT!

The road to *spiritual maturity* is strewn with many *pitfalls!*

The time for My return is quickly approaching!

♥ My people must be reached!
   ♥ My people must be taught!
      ♥ My people must be forgiven!

I tell you the truth, a time is coming and has now come when the dead will hear the voice of the Son of God and those who hear will live. JOHN 5:25

♥ Who will go to the lost?
   ♥ Who will seek for unbelievers?
      ♥ Who will speak for justice?

When My disciples make themselves available…the Holy Spirit will teach you all what must be told!

We do, however, speak a message of wisdom among the mature, but not the wisdom of this age or of the rulers of this age, who are coming to nothing. No, we speak of God's secret wisdom, a wisdom that has been hidden and that God destined for our glory before time began. None of the rulers of this age understood it, for if they had, they would not have crucified the Lord of glory. 1 CORINTHIANS 2:6

You, dear disciple, will speak of GOD's *secret wisdom!*

This *wisdom* has been hidden…and GOD destined it for *your glory before time began!*

Without the *power* of the Holy Spirit…you can do nothing…*nothing*…in your own strength to further the growth of the Body of Christ—the church!

✝ You, and My chosen, are the church!
✝ You, and My friends—My true friends—are the Body of CHRIST JESUS, your Redeemer!
✝ You, and My people, are a Royal Priesthood…a Chosen People of Almighty GOD…Creator of **you**…in Our Own Image!

However, as it is written:

"No eye has seen, no ear has heard, no mind has conceived what God has

prepared for those who love him"— *but God has revealed it to us by his Spirit.*
1 CORINTHIANS 2:9-10
* Have you been *listening?*
* Have you been *silent?*
* Have you been *faithful?*
* Have you been *joyful* in the face of adversity?
~ Then, cherished one, put on the Mind of Christ...to gain *wisdom, discernment, spiritual insight!*
~ Then, beloved soul, put on the Heart of Christ... to *love without conditions...forgive all sins and hurts* against you!
~ Then, treasured spirit, put on the Wisdom of Christ... to *see, feel, and hear*...what is happening in the *spiritual dimensions*...and *know secrets* beyond the earthly and worldly realms!
~ Then, chosen soul, put on the Spirit of Christ...to understand the Word of GOD...and *unite with Our Warrior Angels*; and in the *Power of the Holy Spirit*...praying for GOD's perfect Will to be manifested for everyone around the world...families...friends...and foe, alike!

!ALL TO THE GLORY OF ELOHIM!

My people, My true, My chosen, My faithful, My obedient...bear Spiritual Fruit...each day of their lives...wherever they are...and in whatever they are doing...whenever they are intent on the things and commands of EL GIBBOR...GOD ALMIGHTY!

The *tongue* can be an evil and mighty tool...when given over to the plans of Satan...Enemy of GOD and His people!

The *ears* can be infiltrated with evil and foul language...when *tuning* the Enemy's voice in...and *tuning* GOD out!

These are choices each man, woman and child must make every moment of every day!

Every person's eyes, ears and mind...can be assaulted by Satan most easily in these last days!

Do not merely listen to the word, and so deceive yourselves. Do what it says. JAMES 1:22

But the man who looks intently into the perfect law that gives freedom, and continues to do this, nor forgetting what he has heard, but doing it—he will be blessed in what he does. JAMES 1:25

† Come...Blessed One!
† Come...Faithful Friend!
† Come...Boldly to ABBA!

† Come...Willingly to CHRIST!
  † Come...Filled with the HOLY SPIRIT!
Once you were not a people, but now you are the people of God; once you had
not received mercy, but now you have received mercy. 1 PETER 2:10
JEHOVAH-M'Kaddesh, your Sanctifier,
LOVES YOU BEYOND MEASURE!

Your Eternal Friend,
  Yeshua ha'Machiach

Precious Sweet-one:

If anyone considers himself religious and yet does not keep a tight rein
on his tongue, he deceives himself and his religion is worthless.
Religion that God our Father accepts as pure and faultless
is this: to look after orphans and widows in their distress
and to keep oneself from being polluted by the world.
JAMES 1:26-27

! HE LOVES ME...
HE LOVES ME NOT !

The LORD has dealt with me
according to my righteousness;
according to the cleanness of my
hands he has rewarded me.
For I have kept the ways of the LORD;
I have not done evil by turning from my God.
All his laws are before me;
I have not turned away from his decrees.
I have been blameless before him
and have kept myself from sin.
the LORD has rewarded me according
to my righteousness,
according to the cleanness of my
hands in his sight.
To the faithful you show yourself faithful,
to the blameless you show yourself blameless,
to the pure you show yourself pure,
but to the crooked you show yourself shrewd.
You save the humble
but bring low those whose eyes are haughty.
PSALM 18:20-27

Those whom I love I rebuke and discipline.
So be earnest and repent.
REVELATION 3:19

O' My Dearest Friend,

LISTEN closely for My Voice in your heart and soul...through the power of the HOLY SPIRIT!

This message contains more *secrets* regarding **My Love for you**...and **your love for Me**!

I hear your thoughts, 'What *more* can the LORD tell me about love?'

'Why does He speak *constantly* of *unconditional love*? Even for our enemies...which is *difficult*, and many times, *impossible*!'

Whoever does not love does not know God, because God is love. 1 JOHN 4:8

Have you truly understood what John has written?

These words have not come through *his human heart*!

These words have come through *his spiritual heart*...even from his *soul*...through his *mind*...because he has been Born-Again and *filled completely* with the *wisdom, knowledge,* and *understanding* from the HOLY SPIRIT!

- ♥ Without the Spirit of the Living GOD...there would **not** be **true** and **pure** love!
- ♥ Without the Spirit of the Living GOD...there would **not** be **desire** to love and be loved!
- ♥ Without the Spirit of the Living GOD...there would **not** be *willingness* to **love** and **forgive** unconditionally!

Above all, love each other deeply, because love covers over a multitude of sins. 1 PETER 4:8

Where has LOVE come from?

Not from Satan...who is not only the *symbol* of hate and destruction...he IS HATE!

The more *My LOVE*...the LOVE you shower on others because GOD Almighty first loved you...the angrier the Enemy and his cohorts become, and the more determined they are to destroy the LOVE through evil thoughts and mind-boggling persuasions!

Who is it that overcomes the world? Only he who believes that Jesus is the Son of God. 1 JOHN 5:5

How many men and women, and even children, do you know, have the terribly mistaken idea that, "GOD can't love me! I am too bad; and if there are people who know me, and hate me...how can GOD even care about me—I'm *insignificant!*"

How many times have you heard someone say, "He just loves *holy* people...those who go to church and do *good* things, and are always *nice* to others!"

"I would have to change a lot, before GOD can even *like* me—or even know I exist!"

- † Are **not** all these just **excuses**?
- † Are **not** all these thoughts...denying who GOD truly is?
- † Are **not** these statements born out of *spiritual ignorance*?

O cherished friend, **you** must tell them for Me...the Father—their Creator—has given MERCY and GRACE!

His Mercy and Grace were manifested through His Only Begotten SON—JESUS! The Promised MESSIAH!

I, JESUS, shed My Blood, to pay the full price of Redemption—for any Jew or Gentile—who would accept Me, who would be My disciple, My beloved Bride! They will sit at the Banquet Table reserved for them!

You, beloved, who has been Born-Again, are a saint and one of My dearest friends!

Jesus replied,

"If anyone loves me, he will obey my teaching. My Father will love him, and we will come to him and make our home with him. He who does not love me will not obey my teaching. These words you hear are not my own; they belong to the Father who sent me. JOHN 14:23-24

This is one of Our *Heavenly Secrets*, dear one!

When your time on Earth is over...you will be in Our Presence!

There is Eternity to learn and understand all that is too difficult to grasp with your *human mind*...and that which you can not *see* with *human sight*...and *hear* all you can not hear with *human ears*!

- ♥ See...with your HEART!
- ♥ Listen...with your SOUL!
- ♥ Look...with your SPIRIT!

When you were born from your mother's womb...your life took human form in an earthly world!

When you were born into the Heavenly Dimension...you were filled by the Holy Spirit for the Spirit Life within you!

- * As you *grow* in your knowledge of the Father...the Son...and the Holy Spirit...you are *seeing* both GOOD and EVIL!
- * As you *mature* in your spiritual life...you will *desire* to enter Heaven more...and be in the world...even less!
- * As you *draw* closer to the LORD of lords...the world goes farther and farther away!

However, through Supernatural Self-Control, Obedience and Faithfulness...will you realize how much We love you!

The world you are in, right now...is not your destiny!

The world you are in, right now...is in an agony of its own making!

! **Rejoice**...that you are only **in this world** ... but **not of it**!

! **Rejoice**...that I came **willingly** to **redeem** all whom the Father gave Me!

! **Rejoice**...that you were **blessed** with the ability to **relinquish** your *free will* to Me...you are **Mine**!

Tell others of My deep love for each of them...just as they are!

- ♥ Open your *spiritual eyes* to see all that I accomplish for you each day!

♥ Open your *spiritual ears* to hear what I whisper in your heart!

♥ Open your *spiritual mind* to know, discern, and understand the things of GOD to protect and guide you!

SING PRAISES TO GOD ALL YOU WHO LOVE HIM!

SHOUT WITH JOY TO THE GOD OF ABRAHAM, ISAAC, AND JACOB!

RAISE YOUR ARMS TO THE HEAVENS, AND PROCLAIM YOUR BELIEF IN THE KING OF kings!

My LOVE is Beyond Measure…
For My Beloved Bride…
Who Waits Patiently For Me!

The Lover Of Your Soul,
Jesus, The LORD

! WHY DO YOU 'UPSET' ME? !

Who is a God like you, who pardons sin and forgives the
transgression of the remnant of his inheritance?
You do not stay angry forever but delight to show mercy.
You will again have compassion on us; you will tread our sins
underfoot and hurl all our iniquities into the depths of the sea.
You will be true to Jacob, and show mercy to Abraham, as
you pledged on earth to our fathers in days long ago.
MICAH 7:18-20

You see, at just the right time, when we were still
powerless, Christ died for the ungodly.
Very rarely will anyone die for a righteous man, though for
a good man someone might possibly dare to die.
But God demonstrates his own love for us in this:
While we were still sinners, Christ died for us.
ROMANS 5:6-8

O' My Dearest Disciple,

You have much work to do in these *last days*!

† Are you not aware, as to what your LORD, and My angels, are *seeing* from the heavenlies?

† Are you not aware, of the terrible and horrible immorality, idolatry, and hypocrisy that are *rampant* all over the world?

† Are you not aware, as to the *sinfulness* in your own household…in your **own life**?

'But, LORD', you cry out! I know I am 'sinning'…but they are only *small sins!*'

'Yes', my child! As soon as you turn around, **wherever** you might be, you have NOT *strengthened* your SPIRITUAL MIND, HEART, and SOUL to handle the temptations that may **suffocate you**!

Those may fill you with *overwhelming fear*, as well!

'But, LORD, I can handle myself! After all, I have *plenty* of time to do the 'holy' thing! And *really*, LORD! I just want to have a little bit of fun! You know, LORD, each person, including me…has a FREE WILL!'

O, dear child! Do you not know that **your sins**…each one…nailed ME to the Cross?

The Father *created YOU*, to be part of a *holy* and *chosen* people…to bring Him GLORY!

For you are a people holy to the LORD your God. The LORD your God has chosen you out of all the peoples on the face of the earth to be his people, his treasured possession. DEUTERONOMY 7:6

The Almighty LORD has sanctified you…set you apart for **His divine service!**

How could YOU NOT ACCEPT this calling…from the ELOHIM HIMSELF?!

Remember when you were a child! There were many games you liked to play…and these games meant that there had to be *two teams*…one against the other!

Remember how excited everyone was? Remember how one *specific* child was always CHOSEN to be the leader of each team?

Remember how much fun it was to be CHOSEN for your favorite group of *friends*? Everyone shouting, 'Choose me!' 'Choose me!'

Then the leader began the selections! Then the sadness on the faces of those who were waiting, after the leaders chose their 'favorite' team members!

How many times were you among the last few? Waiting? Still waiting?

Then, sighs of resignation from the leaders! 'Okay!' they thought! 'We have to choose from these last ones!'

The leaders would give each other a look! As if to say, 'all right! I'll take the one on the left! You take the one on the right!'

Then, your name was called out!

You felt the 'saddest excitement'…as did the other child! Tears were burning behind your eyes!

'What is *wrong* with me?' You are thinking! 'Am I *never good enough*? I am so **angry**, I'd like to run home and stay there!'

However, you stay! And you play the best you can!

Dearest and cherished! Perhaps you will find JOY in knowing that your LORD will **never** UPSET you! Though your sins can *upset* ME…I will continue to CHOOSE YOU to be on My Team!

- ♥ When you cry to ME…you are saved!
- ♥ When you trust in ME…you will **not** be disappointed!

> *When I am afraid,*
> *I will trust in you.*
> *In God, whose word I praise,*
> *In God I trust; I will not be afraid.*
> *What can mortal man do to me?*
> PSALM 56:3-4

People…may reject and disappoint you…many times over!

Never think, nor assume, these rejections or disappointments, are coming from the Master!

ANY THING, ANY CIRCUMSTANCE, ANY SELFISH or **SELF-SERVING ACT** that is negative, can not come, nor originate from the *dimensions* in the heavens!

! I AM PURE OF HEART!

You must understand this Truth…and *rejoice in* it *immediately*!

♥ Hide yourself in Me!

♥ Stand in My Shadow!

♥ Stay in My Presence!

The days of the blameless are known to the LORD, and their inheritance will endure forever. PSALM 37:18

Come to Me! Renounce any and all negative thoughts! Do NOT allow these to *lead* you into sin!

Why would you…My chosen child…desire to UPSET Me?

Come to Me! Seek *strength* from My Holy Spirit, so you *can* turn your face from the Enemy's temptation!

Learn to recognize these temptations that will lead you into sin: Spiritually! Mentally! Emotionally! Physically! Financially!

If you are surprised that you can sin in any one of these ways…do not be!

Seek righteousness through your Faith in ME…JESUS, your LORD!

Do NOT allow anyone to *confuse* you in your sin! Many, who follow the world, will tell you that 'sinning is only human'! However, being 'only human' is not giving a child of the Most High GOD the approval to continue in your sins!

I, the LORD of lords, love you *unconditionally*…just as *you* are to love others!

It is the **SIN which UPSETS** your LORD!

Through the Baptism of the Holy Spirit…you are Sanctified…and live in My GRACE and MERCY!

I, the KING of kings, LOVE YOU BEYOND MEASURE!

♥ YOU ARE THE JOY OF MY ETERNITY! ♥

There is no one who could ever make this Divine Statement…**no one**!

Your Blessedness Forever!

The Son of the Most High and Only One True God,

Jesus, the Messiah

! HOW SMART ARE YOU? !

"Now therefore, listen to me, my children,
For blessed are those who keep my ways.
Hear instruction and be wise,
And do not disdain it.
Blessed is the man who listens to me,
Watching daily at my gates,
Waiting at the posts of my doors.
For whoever finds me finds life,
And obtains favor from the LORD;
But he who sins against me wrongs his own soul;
All those who hate me love death."
PROVERBS 8:32-36 NKJV

Get wisdom! Get understanding!
Do not forget, nor turn away from the words of my mouth.
Do not forsake her, and she will preserve you;
Love her, and she will keep you.
PROVERBS 4:5-6 NKJV

O' My Faithful and Obedient Disciple,
What shall your LORD *teach* you?
What shall your GOD *show* you?
What shall your SAVIOR *say* to you?
Have I not taught you much, through My prophets; through My scribes; through My other willing messengers?

† Have you not *listened?*
† Have you not *heard?*
† Have you not *received?*

I, EL GIBBOR, Almighty GOD, Am He…Who holds nothing back to assist you in your *spiritual* growth!

I can only do this, if *you*, dear one, are *willing* and *available*!

I can *not* do this, however, if your heart is not ready to receive instruction along with wisdom!

Solomon, himself, in all his earthly riches…considered WISDOM greater than any earthly jewel; more than any earthly goal!

David also reached for heavenly instruction; though he failed many times, because of his natural desires; however, he always returned to the GOD of his fathers!

His words always blessed Me!

> *I will bless the LORD who has given me counsel;*
> *My heart also instructs me in the night seasons.*
> *I have set the LORD always before me;*
> *Because He is at my right hand I shall not be moved.*

PSALM 16:7-8 NKJV

Do you, dear heart, desire to accept instruction from your LORD of lords?

When have you sought Me?

…Only when trouble is near?

…Secretly in the dead of night?

…Joyfully after a good night's rest in sleep?

Tell Me, precious one, when do you seek your KING of kings for **wisdom?**

After you have failed once, or a few times?

Are you *seeking wisdom* from Me now?

Yes, dear one!

You have prayed, have you not?

Because you are hearing or reading this message, blessed disciple, means you have sought your LORD Redeemer, for *wise counsel!*

You have worked toward much *spiritual strength* to make **your heart ready** to hear My Voice!

Even though the cacophony that surrounds you…you, dearest one, have focused only on *My Voice!*

You have turned your ear to the Power of the HOLY SPIRIT!

There are too many voices which will desire to claim your attention!

Remember this, dearest disciple, the Enemy uses any one and any means possible to distract My messengers from their Divine Assignments!

Give instruction to a wise man, and he will be still wiser; Teach a just man, and he will increase in learning. PROVERBS 9:9 NKJV

Are you a 'just man', or a 'just woman', O faithful one?

Loving others, *unconditionally,* makes you 'just'…does it not?

Are you able to *love* for My sake…without seeking a reward?

"How does loving others for you, LORD, earn me a reward?" you wonder!

"Did you not say to *love* others as you want others to *love* you, LORD?" you also wonder!

"I desire to love others, LORD, to bring GLORY to the FATHER!" you say to Me!

♥ Is this 'just'?
　♥ Is this 'righteous'?
　　♥ Is this 'obedience'?
　　　♥ Is this 'faithfulness'?

These are not *choice* questions, dear one!

You are 'obedient'…when you seek after 'righteousness'…and then you are 'just'…which are all in 'faithfulness' to EL GIBBOR—GOD Almighty's Commandments!

JEHOVAH-tsidkenu **is** your righteousness!

Being righteous…you seek after justice!

+ Does this make you more *intelligent* than others?
+ Do you *judge* the knowledge of others and seek only to be in their company?
+ Do you see more *Wisdom* in those who have…or profess to have… intelligence and knowledge?

Or, because of *spiritual discernment* and *spiritual insight* from the Holy Spirit…you see more Wisdom in a child, a simple man or woman, or in an elderly person?!

This, dear one, is TRUE WISDOM of a CHRIST-follower!

Desiring to please GOD—rather than man—makes you a person after My own heart, blessed one!

> *"The fear of the LORD is the beginning of wisdom,*
> *And the knowledge of the Holy One is understanding.*
> *For by me your days will be multiplied,*
> *And years of life will be added to you.*
> *If you are wise, you are wise for yourself,*
> *And if you scoff, you will bear it alone."*
> PROVERBS 9:10-12 NKJV

Why then, dear one, does the world measure intelligent capabilities?

For each person's glory, is it not?

A child who is not capable to read at the level deemed proper by man… is filled with *wisdom* and *joy* gifted only by GOD Almighty!

ELOHIM—Creator of mankind—has, Himself, given an *anointed measure* of thinking, acting, and reacting…to each and every man, woman and child…which He planned from before the beginning!

Therefore, who has given the world the right to judge?

Is not Satan the god of this world?

Yes…he has placed a veil over men, that makes them *think*
they are superior to each other…even when they are not!
Call upon Me in the day of trouble;
I will deliver you, and you shall glorify Me."
But to the wicked God says:
"What right *have you to declare My statutes,*
Or take My covenant in your mouth,
Seeing you hate instruction
And cast My words behind you?
PSALM 50:15-17 NKJV
Therefore, dear and anointed disciple, come to Me in all humility of
thoughts and actions!
Happy is the man who finds wisdom,
And the man who gains understanding;
For her proceeds are better than the profits of silver,
And her gain than fine gold.
She is more precious than rubies,
And all the things you may desire cannot compare
with her. PROVERBS 3:13-15 NKJV
COME TO ME…
BLESSED AND CHERISHED DISCIPLE…
FOR MY LOVE FOR YOU
IS BEYOND MEASURE!

Your Adonai,
Master Teacher,
Jesus, the KING of kings and LORD of lords

! DOES YOUR LORD LOVE YOU? !

"For God so loved the world that he gave his one and only Son, that whoever believes in him shall not perish but have eternal life.
JOHN 3:16

O' My Dearest and Most Blessed of My Creation,

I AM WHO AM, is able to answer those who doubt My Love, by saying:

'I NOT ONLY LOVE YOU...I AM *IN LOVE* WITH YOU'!

Understand this:

† 'I *DIED* FOR YOU'!

† 'I *SHED MY BLOOD* FOR SUCH AS YOU'!

† 'I, ALONE, PAID THE PRICE TO REDEEM YOUR SOUL'!

O dearest disciple! Your LORD has *many missions* for you to accomplish! There are many souls I need you to touch!

Come before your LORD each and every day!

* DO NOT go on with any list of 'things to do' BEFORE coming to present yourself *openly and eagerly* to ME!
* DO NOT come before the LORD of lords...the KING of kings, the PRINCE of the entire KINGDOM and all WORLDS, with lists of '*I want you to do these favors for me*'!

...Always *requests* for 'me'!?

...Always *prayers* for 'me'!?

...Always *give* this or that to 'me'!?

Many of My disciples do not request any thing for any one *else*!

Many have the attitude: 'they can pray and ask for themselves, just like I do'! 'They're just too lazy to pray'!

Many have the attitude: 'Hey, pray to JESUS, He'll do whatever you want'!

Many have the attitude: 'Hey, God helps those who help themselves'! And then swear that line was handed down from the God up there... pointing towards the sky!

Let Me, the ELOHIM, Creator of ALL, tell you of the *wisdom* of those who lived long ago!

~ They knew in their heart of hearts, that an Almighty God existed!

~ They knew in the depths of their souls, that there was someone *Greater* than they were!

~ They knew in the discernment of their minds, that there was, and is, something much better for all of humanity after the body dies!

What of you?

Have you had to be convinced?

One of My dearest servants…in the midst of his vile sins, said:

The fool says in his heart, "There is no God." They are corrupt, and their ways are vile; there is no one who does good. PSALM 53:1

David had to *understand* those words completely, in order to utter them!

And utter them he did! As he cried out to Almighty God…David prostrated himself on the bare ground! His face in the dirt! His arms outstretched!

He watered the dry ground with his tears!

Tears of awakening *wisdom* and *discernment*!

A second time, David cried out to the God of his fathers:

Listen to my prayer, O God, do not ignore my plea; hear me and answer me. PSALM 55:1-2

Have *you*, dear one, cried out to Me, as David did? As so many of My prophets did…and still do?

† They waited for the **PROMISE**!

† Through the **PROMISE**…would be **SALVATION**!

† They accepted the **consequences** of their sins!

> Yet…in MERCY they cried out:
> 'When, O God Most High, will you bring us:
> …the TRUE DELIVERER?
> …the PROMISE?
> …the SAVIOR?
> …the MESSIAH?
> …the ALPHA?
> …the OMEGA?
> …the I AM?'

† They have been visited by the SON and the HOLY SPIRIT!

† They had to wait for the Promised One to sit on His Throne…the KING of kings!

Tell Me…how can people watch, as many Bibles are given to the poor, yet have none of their own?

Or, do have a Bible, but just simply *carry it*…never opening it? Not knowing one word that is written on its pages?

Many times, doing a '*Christian duty*', only to be seen by others?

Sadder still…never experiencing **MY LOVE FOR THEM**?

Do they remind you of when I became enraged, with righteous anger?

Yes! The Pharisees! The Chief Priests! The Sanhedrin!

All those who followed the LETTER OF THE LAW and, at the same time, living life as hypocrites!

Many ask today, 'Is there a God Who truly loves us?' 'Then why is there so much suffering in the world?'

Here is a question for them: 'What are **they** doing to **change** the suffering?'

Ask them: 'Why do they just stand around and **comment** on the woes of the world, instead of rolling up their own sleeves and helping to alleviate suffering…one person at a time?'

Dear ones, perhaps one person in ten *may* answer the call! Perhaps! However, do not *ever* become *discouraged*!

You are to do what your LORD has 'called' and 'chosen' you to do for Him!

Do it! With JOY! With LOVE! Knowing that one day, there will be a wonderful feast in Heaven!

You, dearest and faithful and obedient one, will sit down with ME… the LORD of lords…the KING of kings…together with all the chosen of the Father!

We will feast…while our enemies watch!

- ⁺ Am I **YOUR** *LORD?*
- ⁺ Am I **YOUR** *REDEEMER?*
- ⁺ Am I **YOUR** *SAVIOR?*
- ⁺ Did I not *DIE* for **YOU?**
- ⁺ Did I not **LEAVE MY THRONE IN GLORY** *for YOU?*
- ⁺ Did I not **PROMISE TO RETURN** *for YOU?*

If **YOU** have been able to answer 'Yes, LORD'!, then you are *certain* that your **LORD DOES LOVE YOU!**

- ♥ Whatever the ELOHIM has called you to do…do **all** to His GLORY!
- ♥ Wherever JEHOVAH-nissi has taken you…you **will** be *victorious!*
- ♥ Whenever you feel *alone and abandoned*, JEHOVAH-shammah, is 'ever present', 'always there', **never** leaving nor forsaking you!

Come! As your El-Shaddai…I will supply and nourish you with all you need!

Come! As your Adonai…I will guide and teach you in all you need to do for the GLORY of the FATHER!

I AM HE…WHO LOVES YOU…
BEYOND MEASURE!

Your Beloved,
Yeshua ha'Machiach

! WHY WAIT FOR ME? !

Do you not know?
Have you not heard?
The LORD is the everlasting God,
the Creator of the ends of the earth.
He will not grow tired or weary,
and his understanding no one can fathom.
He gives strength to the weary
and increases the power of the weak.
Even youths grow tired and weary,
and young men stumble and fall;
but those who hope in the LORD
will renew their strength.
They will soar on wings like eagles;
they will run and not grow weary,
they will walk and not be faint.
ISAIAH 40:28-31

O' My Precious Disciple,

The Father wonders if you are *surprised* when I address you as such?

As My precious…you are blessed!

You have been chosen to be an extension of My *arms*, My *smiles*, My *feet*, My *hands*, and My *voice*!

Too difficult to believe these words…My innermost thoughts?

Nothing…NOT ONE THING…is too difficult to believe and accomplish…as long as you **wait** for My blessed instructions!

♥ As long as you remain in My presence…

♥ As long as you rely on My strength…

there is nothing you can not accomplish…as long as it is all done to the GLORY of the FATHER!

Hinder not the 'waiting times'!

These times are not to punish you…as if you were a child!

These times are for the *refreshment* of your body, your mind, your spirit and your soul!

Believe Paul, when he told the people in Philippi:

…I have learned the secret of being content in any and every situation,

whether well fed or hungry, whether living in plenty or in want. I can do everything through him who gives me strength. PHILIPPIANS 4:12-13

'Through Him'! He spoke of ME…the LORD of lords!

'The secret'! He studied My life…Jesus, Son of Man on Earth…and learned of Me!

He tried to emulate the life of the Christ while on Earth!

Are you, dear one, able to *breathe* your LORD into your entire *heart, soul, body, mind* and *spirit*?

You still ask, 'How can I do this'?

LISTEN: to the *whispers* from the Holy Spirit!

"Be still, and know that I am God; I will be exalted among the nations, I will be exalted in the earth." PSALM 46:10

+ BEING STILL…does not mean that you cease from intercessory prayer!
+ BEING STILL…does not mean that you stop doing daily work and chores!
+ BEING STILL…does not mean that you ignore the needs of your loved ones!
+ BEING STILL…does not mean that you stop any of your Blessed Assignments, which I have entrusted to you!

My dearest disciple, My chosen child! Open your spiritual ears and mind to more of David's words,

…and know—understand!

…and know—listen in your heart!

…and know—learn more of your LORD!

† I AM GOD! Acknowledge My **Supremacy**!

† I AM GOD! The only **One** and **True** GOD!

† I AM GOD! Recognize and bow to My **Holiness**!

† I AM GOD! Understand that I Am **Divine**!

† I AM GOD! The **ALPHA** and the **OMEGA**! The beginning and the end…**ETERNAL**!

I AM! I ALWAYS WAS – IS – AND ALWAYS WILL BE!

These are the TRUTHS, which I teach you, as you WAIT UPON ME!

Learn to serve your LORD in even the most mundane of tasks!

♥ Give Me GLORY!

♥ Give Me PRAISE!

♥ Give Me ADORATION!

Do all this, as you wait for the appearance of your Savior!

Remember to come to Me, upon awakening each day!

...I will instruct you, and be with you at every moment!

Remember to speak to Me, at mid day!

...I will continue to uphold you!

Remember to acknowledge My presence as you prepare for your nightly rest!

...I will sit at your side, and not only protect your spirit and soul...as you sleep...I will be LORD of your dreams!

All you have to do...is *ask*!

Listen, cherished disciple! While you 'wait on Me', show My Love and Affection to all whom you meet!

You will encounter those who *repel* you...do not turn your face away!

A smile...while looking straight into their eyes...will do more than you can ever imagine!

As I have told you before, you may meet an angel...or even your LORD!

* Open your eyes wide, and pray to recognize Me!
* Open your heart larger, and allow yourself to love those who are outside of your inner circle!
* Open your mind, and learn more about Me from all that has been written, and is still being written, by inspiration of the Holy Spirit!

You will always know My Holy Spirit is speaking...because the greatest *peace*, and the deepest *love* will envelop you with My own heavenly mantle!

My angels will surround you, and protect you from any doubts which others may use to try to confuse you!

Be ever on the alert...especially when you are waiting for your LORD!

Come! Drink thirstily from My Living Water!

Come! Offer adoration with every fiber of your being!

Come! Look not to the right, nor to the left, nor behind you...keep your eyes and your purpose...straight in front of you!

Watch for My appearing...it will not be long in coming!

My disciples desired to know when I would return, and what will be the sign of the end of the age!

Jesus answered: "Watch out that no one deceives you. For many will come in my name, claiming, 'I am the Christ,' and will deceive many. You will hear of wars and rumors of wars, but see to it that you are not alarmed. Such things must happen, but the end is still to come. MATTHEW 24:4-6

I AM your JEHOVAH-rohi…

the Shepherd…

Who always rescues you, because

I LOVE YOU BEYOND MEASURE!

Your Companion and Friend,
  Jesus, The Christ

Precious **S**weet-one:

> *I tell you the truth, this generation will certainly not pass away until all things have happened. Heaven and earth will pass away, but my words will never pass away.*
> MATTHEW 24:34-35

! I WILL ANSWER... MY WAY !

My flesh and my heart may fail,
but God is the strength of my heart
and my portion forever.
Those who are far from you will perish;
you destroy all who are unfaithful to you.
But as for me, it is good to be near God.
I have made the Sovereign LORD my refuge;
I will tell of all your deeds.
PSALM 73:26-28

Whom have I in heaven but you?
And earth has nothing I desire besides you.
PSALM 73:25

O' My Dearest and Precious Child,

The Father is pleased with all the blessed promises you have made… especially in times of utter distress!

Many cry out to GOD only when 'life' has tossed them to-and-fro!

Many never even mention My Name, then they wonder why circumstances do not change!

Their 'lives'…minds and hearts…are then ripe for the Enemy and his cohorts to move into their circles! Then, dear child, they think they are being surrounded by 'good luck'!

They know not, that the Almighty God of the Universe, does not give 'good luck' nor 'bad luck'! They are completely blinded to the Truth!

What of you? You make promises to your LORD God!

When you are put to the test…

…Do you *stand* on My Word?

…Do you *continue* to exhibit your trust in the Almighty?

…Do you *bow* your spirit before Me?

…Do you *live* and *walk* in the steps of your Redeemer?

♥ Remember, My child, when you prostrated before Me, in true repentance?

♥ Remember, when you gave your mind, heart, soul, spirit and body completely to the LORD of lords?

♥ Remember, when you said, 'I am available, sweet Jesus, for *whatever You desire* for me to do?' You became a 'new creation' in Me!

Those you love, who had already experienced the New Birth, shouted praises and worshipped your KING!

However, the others did not like, nor understood the change in you!

Then you gave even more of yourself to Me! You *promised to accept whatever I allowed*, in order for 'unsaved' loved ones to accept the Free Gift of Salvation! Also, you continue to pray for those who said the 'sinner's prayer', in the past…and wait for them to be filled with the *Holy Spirit!*

You, blessed child, offered your life! You became 'crucified with your Christ', when you vowed this most anointed promise!

Because of this, I took you at your word!

… You learned to pray in the power of the Holy Spirit!

… You came with holy boldness into the Throne Room!

… You approached the Father, in My Name!

… You said to the Father: 'Thy will be done'!

… You prayed with total trust!

When you became weak and unable to control any situation in your personal life…the Father had Me offer My Divine Intervention!

The Holy Spirit spoke these words through Paul:

… *"My grace is sufficient for you, for my power is made perfect in weakness."*
2 CORINTHIANS 12:9

That is why, My friend, for My sake…you delighted in weaknesses, in insults, in hardships, in persecutions, in difficulties! For when *you* are weak…then I am strong!

This is the true witness, My friend!

This is when you are following in the footsteps of your LORD and KING!

When you are in need—whether in the spirit, in your emotions, in your physical body, or in your poverty—you, My chosen disciple, are still filled with My Joy!

♥ You shine with My love!

♥ You pray with praises and adoration!

♥ You give freely out of your own needs…to bless others who may call you a fool!

♥ You continue to forgive, especially, when others take advantage of you!

♥ You are unaware of how many 'seeds' you are planting for My Name's sake!

There are many times, when you have cried out to Me, in the darkness of the night!

When My heart was grieved and my spirit embittered, I was senseless and ignorant; I was a brute beast before you. Yet I am always with you; you hold me by my right hand. You guide me with your counsel, and afterward you will take me into glory. PSALM 73:21-24

✝ Remember…there is no emotion I do not understand!

✝ I experienced all, during My time away from Glory!

✝ I accepted any request from our ABBA!

I cried out in a loud voice, "Eloi, Eloi, lama sabachthani?"—"My God, my God, why have you forsaken me?"…when I was in *agony* hanging on the Cross!

However, Elohim did not forsake Me!

Neither will I, the Christ, ever leave or forsake My friends…My disciples!

I drank the Cup! Many of you, also, drank the Cup, which I offered to you!

On Earth, the time as you know it, seems slow and long!

Do not fear, nor fret!

The Joy in Heaven, will be that much more glorious! Because it will be for Eternity with your LORD!

Come! I will comfort and bless you!

I AM THE LORD AND KING OF GLORY…
WHO LOVES YOU BEYOND MEASURE!

Jesus

Precious Sweet-one:

Praise be to the LORD God, the God of Israel,
who alone does marvelous deeds.
Praise be to his glorious name forever;
may the whole earth be filled with his glory.
Amen and Amen.
PSALM 72:18-19

! WHAT IS YOUR SACRIFICE? !

*Through Jesus, therefore, let us continually offer to God a sacrifice of
praise—the fruit of lips that confess his name. And do not forget to do
good and to share with others, for with such sacrifices God is pleased.*
HEBREWS 13:15-16

But Samuel replied:
*"Does the LORD delight in burnt offerings and sacrifices as
much as in obeying the voice of the LORD? To obey is better
than sacrifice, and to heed is better than the fat of rams.*
1 SAMUEL 15:22

O' My Precious Disciple,

The Father desires *praises*, true *worship* and pure *adoration*, from His
Creation of man and woman in His Image!

However, there is another action He desires from you, and all who
accept Me as His Son...to accept and recognize the Father...for Who He
Is! Then, to accept and see Me...for Who I Am!

*"Do not let your hearts be troubled. Trust in God; trust also in me. In my
Father's house are many rooms; if it were not so, I would have told you. I am
going there to prepare a place for you. And if I go and prepare a place for you,
I will come back and take you to be with me that you also may be where I am.
You know the way to the place where I am going."* JOHN 14:1-4

Now, dear disciple, I, JESUS, Whom you now know as The Christ,
spoke the words, which John recorded, in the hearing of the Eleven! Judas
had already left the upper room!

I had only a short time, to tell them what was about to happen!

When each disciple promised to lay down his life for Me...I had to tell
Peter, that he would betray Me that very night!

Peter had come a very long way in his spiritual walk...by following his
LORD...for over three years! He knew whatever I told him was true, and
would happen just as I said it would!

What of you? Have you learned to believe every word I have said to
you?

Thomas and Philip were also with Me for three years! Yet, they kept
saying to Me, that they did not know where I was going! Thomas still asked
Me, "We do not know where you're going. How *could* we know the way?"

Then, Philip also kept asking Me, 'Show us the Father, and that will be enough'!

All the apostles were becoming very quiet that night!

I ask again, dear one, 'Do you not believe that I am in the Father…and that the Father is in Me?'

He is living in Me…doing His work and the miracles through Me!

Do you realize, that *believing* in the existence of GOD, the Father, that He sent His one and only Son to Earth, as a sacrifice for YOU…is a *miraculous mystery?*

He is the atoning sacrifice for our sins, and not only for ours but also for the sins of the whole world. 1 JOHN 2:2

You are blessed, when you follow the examples of your LORD of lords, and the lives of My first chosen apostles and disciples!

"A new command I give you: Love one another. As I have loved you, so you must love one another. By this all men will know that you are my disciples, if you love one another." JOHN 13:34-35

The sacrifices you have made, and will continue to make, to love each other…*as I have loved you*…will take much strength!

I asked the Father, to give you another Counselor, Who is the Holy Spirit! He will always help you! He is the Spirit of Truth!

However, the world will not accept Him!

Therefore, this spiritual strength will come in your reliance on the Holy Spirit!

Your life, and the lives of all who do accept My Holy Spirit…will never be the same!

- ♥ You will desire to PRAISE, WORSHIP and ADORE the Father!
- ♥ You will desire to offer up SACRIFICES OF PRAISE for any and all pain, which you endure while on Earth!

These Sacrifices of Praise will be for all you suffer…even *anguish* over unsaved loves ones, family, friends, and strangers around the world!

WORSHIP ME!

† Offer up a Sacrifice of Praise
at the foot of My Cross!

WORSHIP ME!

† Offer up a Sacrifice of Praise for
financial upheavals and needs!

WORSHIP ME!

† Offer up a Sacrifice of Praise
for the loss of loved ones!

WORSHIP ME!

✝ Offer up a Sacrifice of Praise
for unrelenting physical pain!

WORSHIP ME!

✝ Offer up a Sacrifice of Praise
for loved ones who live immoral lives!

WORSHIP ME!

✝ Offer up a Sacrifice of Praise
for anything or anyone who hurts you!

WORSHIP ME!

✝ Offer up a Sacrifice of Praise
for watching a loved one suffer from illness,
sins of the flesh, ungodly companions!

WORSHIP ME!

Yes, My dearest disciple! Do not hang your head in 'self-pity'...which comes straight from the Enemy's pit of hell!

Instead...as life's problems assault you...raise your arms up to the sky! With a loud voice...shout words of PRAISE and WORSHIP to your GOD and KING!

Learn to Praise your LORD...in whatever situation you are in!

Learn to sing songs of Worship to your KING...wherever you are!

Do not be ashamed! Remember...others are not embarrassed to shout out obscenities!

Remember to Whom you belong!

You have been chosen before the creation of the world...before earthly time began!

Worshipping the LORD of lords, the KING of kings, thwarts the plans of the Enemy!

Ascribe to the LORD, O mighty ones,
ascribe to the LORD glory and strength.
Ascribe to the LORD the glory due his name;
worship the LORD in the splendor of his holiness.

PSALM 29:1-2

♥ Shout Glory to God!

♥ Sing Alleluia to the KING of Glory!

♥ Offer Thanksgiving to the Holy Spirit!

♥ Pray to the LORD in Adoration!

AMEN! AMEN! AMEN!

Love the LORD your GOD...

**as HE LOVES YOU…
BEYOND MEASURE!**
You, cherished disciple, will be My joy, forever!

Your Beloved,
Christ Jesus

! AM I NOT ENOUGH? !

YESHUA

ELOHIM*EL ELYON
JEHOVAH ADONAI*EL-SHADDAI
JEHOVAH-jireh * JEHOVAH-rophe
JEHOVAH-M'Kaddesh *JEHOVAH-nissi
JEHOVAH-shalom
JEHOVAH-tsidkenu
JEHOVAH-shammah
JEHOVAH-rohi
MESSIAH * CHRIST

O' My Most Precious Disciple,

How many ways the Father loves you! Too many for your human mind to comprehend!

He sent ME...His only Begotten Son...to rescue you, your family, friends, and anyone for whom you pray, to claim for the Kingdom of Heaven!

Yes, to save all who believe...to live in an Eternal Paradise...**not** for eternal Hell!

How much have **I loved you**?

I spent agonizing hours nailed to the Cross...for the Father's Creation! At His request! Did I not?

Have I left you destitute? Alone? In despair? Easy prey for the ravages of the Enemy's claws?

As the Father has offered His Son for you...paying the heavy price of Salvation...I, the Christ, offer you the Holy Spirit!

The Holy Spirit...always ready to help you speak to the Father...in the Name of JESUS...the Son!

The Holy Spirit will guide you...as you accept His in-filling...and become Born Again!

He will guide you on the narrow path, through life on this Earth!

† What **JOY**!

   † What **GRACE**!

      † What **PEACE**!

         † What **VISION**!

Such compelling desire fills you to offer PRAISE, WORSHIP, and ADORATION to…

…♥ The LORD of lords!

…♥ The KING of kings!

…♥ The Redeemer!

…♥ The Sanctifier!

…♥ Yeshua…the Messiah…to Whom Elohim gave the Keys of the Kingdom!

YOU…dearly beloved, are the greatest treasure the Father created!

Listen carefully, O man!

Open your heart, O woman!

Tell of all My wondrous deeds!

Be exalted, O LORD, in your strength; we will sing and praise your might. PSALM 21:13

May he give you the desire of your heart and make all your plans succeed. PSALM 20:4

I will extol the LORD at all times; his praise will always be on my lips. My soul will boast in the LORD; let the afflicted hear and rejoice. Glorify the LORD with me; let us exalt his name together. PSALM 34:1-3

The Father smiles down upon those of His Creation…who see His Son…as their true Treasure!

✝ Do you tell, of how truly difficult it is, to follow in the footsteps of the Christ?

✝ Do you tell, of how there are tears of Joy, in the midst of any pain you experience?

Beware, dearest friend, of those who 'paint' only a pretty picture, to lure others into a supposedly Christian life, but who themselves are not living it!

Then…when these same 'innocent lambs' experience all sorts of evil bombardments from the Enemy…those same ones, who spoke glowingly of the Christian walk…are nowhere to be found for 'unconditional' support!

Remember, by their *spiritual fruits* they…and you…shall be known!

Not as a farmer grows trees that produce figs, nor grapes from the vine!

No earthly fruit will ever compare to the Fruits of the Spirit: Love – Joy – Peace – Patience – Kindness – Goodness – Faithfulness – Gentleness – Self-control! GALATIANS 5-22 (paraphrased)

♥ You, O son and daughter of the KING…must live by the Spirit!

♥ You have crucified the sinful nature, with all its passions and desires, and now belong to Christ Jesus!

Be humble of heart and mind!

What do you *know* of your Savior?

> How do you *understand* your Savior?
>> Why do you *follow* your Savior?
>>> When do you *question* your Savior?

Are you sincere, regarding your Christian walk? Honest? Truthful?

My cherished child, these words are not just for you! They are also for others to whom you are sent...then the Holy Spirit will give you 'discernment' of what to say to them for Me!

Do not go before He has truly guided you!

YOU MUST LISTEN TO ALL I SAY TO YOU!

Telling those who are not prepared...neither spiritually, nor emotionally...can do more *harm* than good! *Their hearts must be ready to receive what you will tell them!*

It is at these times, when the Enemy and his cohorts come in like an evil flood! Then, it will be so much more difficult for them to see the Truth... through the damage the Enemy wreaked in their minds and hearts!

Follow in My footsteps!

Always arm yourself with the Truth from My Holy Scriptures!

Remember...always remember...it is by GRACE you have been saved... through FAITH which comes from the HOLY SPIRIT...Who will bless you with Spiritual Insight...you just simply have to ask!

This is the Gift of GOD! You can not *work* for it.

For it is by grace you have been saved, through faith—and this not from yourselves, it is the gift of God—not by works, so that no one can boast. For we are God's workmanship, created in Christ Jesus to do good works, which God prepared in advance for us to do. EPHESIANS 2:8-10

Tell others, how you have learned...through much suffering...that I, your LORD, have become your ALL-IN-ALL!

Have you, as yet, not *truly* understood? You must continue to learn how to 'die to self'...if you desire, as much as I desire, for you to be My disciple!

* Teach others from your own personal testimony!
* Teach others that you are now, and still are, growing ever closer to your LORD!
* Teach others through My Holy Scriptures!

Our ABBA created the human brain to never stop absorbing new knowledge and understanding…in all aspects of the spirit, the mind, and the heart!

In Heaven, the ever-expanding experiences are filled with JOY, PEACE, HAPPINESS and LAUGHTER, all in the Presence of the HOLY BLESSED TRINITY!

Though you have extended yourself to come closer in knowing your KING…there is so much more growth, which is needed, and necessary!

What most pleases the Father, is when I tell Him how you have grown… especially in your love and adoration of His Son!

Pray, dear one, each day, to put on the *mind* and *heart* of Christ!

† There is much work to be done!

† There are many souls to reach!

† There is much to learn and many to teach…before My return!

Will *you* be ready? Will you?

Come! Take My hand, so we can walk together in My garden!

Come! Close your eyes and sense My Presence!

Come! Let us bow before the Father's Throne and join the Angelic Choir singing songs of worship and adoration to His Wonderful Name!

Always remember…**with Me alone…you have more than enough!**

! YOU ARE LOVED BEYOND MEASURE!

Your ALL-IN-ALL,
 Yeshua ha'Machiach

Precious Sweet-One:

> *"This, then, is how you should pray:*
> *" 'Our Father in heaven,*
> *hallowed be your name,*
> *your kingdom come,*
> *your will be done*
> *on earth as it is in heaven.*
> *Give us today our daily bread.*
> *Forgive us our debts,*
> *as we also have forgiven our debtors.*
> *And lead us not into temptation,*
> *but deliver us from the evil one.'*
> MATTHEW 6:9-13

! IS YOUR SOUL MINE !

Praise the LORD, O my soul;
all my inmost being, praise his holy name.
Praise the LORD, O my soul,
and forget not all his benefits—
who forgives all your sins
and heals all your diseases,
who redeems your life from the pit
and crowns you with love and compassion,
who satisfies your desires with good things
so that your youth is renewed like the eagle's.
PSALM 103:1-5

O' My Dearest Beloved Soul,

Do not be surprised that I am greeting you with these words!

It is for you, that preparations are being made in Heaven…in anticipation of your arrival! In anticipation that you will pass these words on to those whom the Holy Spirit will lead you and others, to testify to the Truth!

♥ I, your LORD, address these words to you:

♥ I Am JESUS, Who is the Christ!

♥ I Am the CHRIST, Who is the Redeemer!

♥ I Am, the REDEEMER, Who is the Truth!

♥ I Am, the TRUTH, Who traverses the Earth, for My "Beloved Souls"!

The souls…which the Elohim created in Our image!

The souls…whom El-Elyon, Our Mighty GOD…gave to Me upon My return into Heaven…as the Son of GOD!

He gave *the chosen* to Me…because of My obedience and faithfulness to leave My Throne and the Joys of Heaven…to come into a world filled with sins of every kind…and redeem those who would **believe** in the **Truth** of the Risen Christ! And anoint those who give up their Free Will to the RISEN CHRIST, their SAVIOR!

Each member of creation has a choice!

You understand, that I, the LORD, *chose you?*

You did not choose me, but I chose you and appointed you to go and bear fruit—fruit that will last. Then the Father will give you whatever you ask in my name. This is my command: Love each other. JOHN 15:16-17

NOW…the choice you must make…is to return your soul to the Father…or to follow Lucifer and his fallen angels into the pit of eternal damnation!

Just as I told My first disciples, I tell you…I ask you…to listen!

! Hear Me, O Beloved Soul of Created Man!

! Hear Me, O Beloved Soul of Created Woman!

Your LORD, your GOD, has not stopped speaking; nor has the ADONAI stopped teaching!

What good will it be for a man if he gains the whole world, yet forfeits his soul? Or what can a man give in exchange for his soul? For the Son of Man is going to come in his Father's glory with his angels, and then he will reward each person according to what he has done. I tell you the truth, some who are standing here will not taste death before they see the Son of Man coming in his kingdom."
MATTHEW 16:26-28

Do these words seem as if they were said, only to My first disciples?

These words were heard by human ears, as they all sat or stood around your LORD!

However, I have had the Holy Spirit inspire those souls who would be *obedient, faithful* and would make themselves *available* to pass them on from one generation to another!

Now…they have been written again…so that you, the reader of today… who desires to become My disciple…will know without any doubts…that My words are meant for men and women *in and for* all ages! FOR ALL TIMES!

…They are meant especially for these 'last days'!

…Read them again! Understand them fully!

…Tell others, and make disciples of all souls…in all nations!

…Baptize them in the Name of the Father…the Son…and the Holy Spirit!

Extend to all…My Grace! My Mercy!

- ♥ Pray, My beloved souls…for *words of wisdom* to encourage acts of *unconditional love*!
- ♥ Pray, My beloved souls…for *words of truth* to change minds and hearts!
- ♥ Pray, My beloved souls…for *words of worship* to sing with devotion!
- ♥ Pray, My beloved souls…for *words to invite many* to come and seek Me! For they *will find Me*…in the most unexpected places!
- † Tell other souls…that the way to follow the LORD of lords…is torturous! It is narrow! It is strewn with pebbles and rocks!

These are the trials to be overcome!

☩ Tell them of My willingness to walk the way of agony…to redeem *all* of the Father's beloved souls!

☩ Tell them, that like you, they *do not belong* on this Earth!

This is why, the yearning for Heaven to be in the presence of the KING…grows deeper and stronger each day!

The Joy of knowing Whom you follow…will overcome the trials and testing you must endure!

However, the Joy which will fill you when you give Me your Free Will… will make it seem as though you are *gliding* over the narrow and rocky path to reach Home!

Do these words instill a desire so deep…so peaceful…so truthful… that you will never allow anything…nor anyone…to remove My love from your beloved soul?

+ Nor from your mind…you will have Knowledge, Wisdom and Understanding!

+ Nor from your spirit…you will have Spiritual Discernment and Insight!

+ Nor from your heart…you will have Truth and Unconditional Love for everyone!

+ Nor from your soul…it will SOAR into My dimension, whenever you desire to spend time with Me!

Imagine visiting the Throne Room! No reservations necessary!

Your Beloved Soul…when it becomes Mine…will bear My Holy Mark!

♥ This Mark will only be seen by others who have also freely given Me their souls!

♥ This Mark will only be seen, as well, by those in the Throne Room, My Angels, My Twelve Apostles and the Leaders of the Tribes; and to anyone I desire to have it revealed!

MIGHTY GOD…EL-ELYON…our JEHOVAH…will be *blessed* and *adored*…to see the legions and legions…who have become My Beloved Souls!

The Light of Heaven will shine upon your faces!

The Enemy and his cohorts will no longer be able to own your souls!

Only the chosen, can look upon each other, and smile in the richness of My Glory…

… Just as the face of Moses glowed, when he descended with the Ten Commandments from Mount Sinai!

…Just as the face of Stephen glowed, when he was being stoned to death…the first Martyr of My disciples!

Understand this: 'the *worldly* and the *spiritual* are many dimensions apart'! The *worldly* can not understand the *spiritual*!

However, the Holy Spirit will give you more wisdom, knowledge, discernment, understanding, and divine insight so you will understand both worlds!

Some of this will happen while in the human body…even more will be learned in your new heavenly body…throughout Eternity!

Do you not know how much you are loved…for these secrets to be revealed to you?

Our Love For You Is Beyond Measure…FOREVER!

I AM WHO AM!
  Y H W H

! JOY AND PEACE DIVINE !

And when you pray, do not keep on babbling like pagans, for they
think they will be heard because of their many words. Do not be like
them, for your Father knows what you need before you ask him.
"This, then, is how you should pray:
" 'Our Father in heaven,
hallowed be your name,
your kingdom come,
your will be done
on earth as it is in heaven.
Give us today our daily bread.
Forgive us our debts,
as we also have forgiven our debtors.
And lead us not into temptation,
but deliver us from the evil one.'
MATTHEW 6:7-13

O' My Most Treasured Disciple,

The Father...your Elohim, the Creator...has heard My prayer for you!

Many are constantly wondering, worrying and woeful, of whether or not Heaven truly exists!

Then the questions...a myriad of questions...arise in the minds and hearts of men, women and even children! These children, who have passed the age of 'spiritual innocence'!

How many times have you read in My Word?:

...He said to them, "Let the little children come to me, and do not hinder them, for the kingdom of God belongs to such as these. MARK 10:14

Heaven is filled with men and women who embraced 'spiritual innocence'!

This does not mean they lacked wisdom, discernment, knowledge or understanding!

This means, that they believed *all* which the Son has shared with them... as coming from the Father, Himself!

I, the LORD, know WHO WILL BE READING OR HEARING THESE WORDS...in these last days!

They have been given to a willing disciple...as I must have...and do have...many willing and faithful disciples all over the Earth...to continue to communicate through the Power of the HOLY SPIRIT, to those whom I have chosen to pass on all that is necessary to prepare for My Return!

- ♥ You, precious child of the KING of kings…are reading or hearing these words, at the exact time of the Father's choosing!
- ♥ You, dear one, are in awe, as to the turn of events in your life, as of this moment!
- ♥ You, cherished soul, are in wonderment, of how much longer you must wait to hear the Trumpet to herald the moment I will return to take My sons and daughters out of this world!

As I have told My people through the Holy Scriptures…through My Messenger Angels…and all other faithful and obedient sons and daughters…'Learn of Me'!

Tell others who will listen, about the Christ JESUS and…

✝ HIS SACRIFICE ✝

✝ HIS LOVE ✝

✝ HIS FORGIVENESS ✝

✝ HIS MERCY ✝

✝ HIS GRACE ✝

As David prayed…you can also pray:

Teach me your way, O LORD, and I will walk in your truth; give me an undivided heart, that I may fear your name. I will praise you, O LORD my God, with all my heart; I will glorify your name forever. PSALM 86:11-12

I must help you to completely understand the most important words of the *Prayer of the LORD*!

Listen…and you will learn another secret Truth of Heaven!

Open your heart and you will be filled with *spiritual wisdom*, which will surpass the understanding of some of the most scholarly and intelligent of men and women upon the Earth! However, this understanding will not escape the mind and heart of a young child!

Each day, millions of people pray 'The LORD's Prayer'!

- ♥ With millions praying the very words I taught to My first disciples… means that people of a different race and color…are **all praying for each other**! Around the countries, around the continents…*around the world*!

Though there is strong disagreement as to man-made church rules…all are in agreement…when beseeching the Father in the same words!

Yet, not all are feeling the same *degree* of *love, forgiveness, joy,* and *peace*!

- ✦ 'hallowed' or holy be Your Name…

- Your Kingdom come…
- Your will be done…
- Not everyone desires for, HIS WILL, to be done on *Earth*…as it is in *Heaven*!

Everything…everywhere…all being done according to the **PERFECT WILL of ELOHIM**!

Is this the way all is done on Earth?

No, dear one, it is not!

Earth was intended for a chosen people…who would live with constant *peace* and unending *joy*!

- Each word spoken by the Father is Divine!
- Each idea thought of by the Father is Divine!
- Each act done by the Father is Divine!

Because of man's disobedience and unfaithfulness, there can be nothing of the Divine Nature on Earth!

When loved ones are called Home to Heaven, this would not cause distress, nor grief…if you could *see* or even *feel* their perfect *peace* and *sublime joy*…which is waiting upon your time to come HOME!

Only those who are not in My Presence…will not experience *peace* nor *joy*!

- ♥ Those who accept My Grace and Mercy…and My Free Gift of Salvation…will be true witnesses of the Divine Peace and Blessed Joy…that are given to those who believe in the One True GOD!

Oh, dearest and precious disciple, continue to seek all which the Holy Spirit has to give you!

When the Glory of the LORD is set free on Earth, as it is in Heaven… HE WILL:

> *Strengthen the feeble hands,*
> *steady the knees that give way;*
> *say to those with fearful hearts,*
> *"Be strong, do not fear;*
> *your God will come,*
> *he will come with vengeance;*
> *with divine retribution*
> *he will come to save you."*
> *Then will the eyes of the blind be opened*
> *and the ears of the deaf unstopped.*
> *Then will the lame leap like a deer,*
> *and the mute tongue shout for joy.*

Water will gush forth in the wilderness
and streams in the desert.
ISAIAH 35:3-6

You are My Treasure, with a value that can not be estimated, because I, the LORD of lords…the KING of kings…**LOVE YOU BEYOND ANY MEASURE!**

Your Messiah,
  Jesus

Precious **S**weet-one:

You will go out in joy
and be led forth in peace;
the mountains and hills
will burst into song before you,
and all the trees of the field
will clap their hands.
ISAIAH 55:12

! BEWARE OF THE ENEMY !

Be self-controlled and alert. Your enemy the devil prowls around like a roaring lion looking for someone to devour. Resist him, standing firm in the faith, because you know that your brothers throughout the world are undergoing the same kind of sufferings.
1 PETER 5:8-9

O' My Most Precious Disciple,
† Can you not *hear?*
† Can you not *see?*
† Can you not *understand* what the Spirit is saying to you?
I must tell you…you must take a stand…and I will stand with you!
Seek My Truth!

Continue to do the Blessed Assignment which I have chosen, just for you! It means much more than you may understand! Even the most menial of tasks could be an *assignment* from your LORD!

Do not fear! I have told you that I will never leave you, nor forsake you! I will be at your side, until I call you Home!

The Enemy is in an uproar…more than he has ever been before!

He has sent his cohorts throughout the world, to stir up evil in every corner, in every walk of life! In every church! In every workplace! In every school! In every government!

There is not one place, that he has not sent his evildoers to stir up trouble!

† BEWARE † † BE AWARE † † BE WARY †

The sting of death is sin, and the power of sin is the law. But thanks be to God! He gives us the victory through our Lord Jesus Christ. 1 CORINTHIANS 15:56-57

…Pray constantly for *spiritual discernment!*
…Understand and be alert!
…Do not allow the Enemy to put his claim into anyone you love!
…Pray for those who do not know Me!
…You have brought many loved ones before Me!
…I know of your love for them…however, *I love them more!* Do you not think this?
…Leave them at the foot of My Cross!
…Pray for those who have no one to pray for them!

…Go out into the highways, and byways *in your prayers* and intercede for those who are lost…spiritually, mentally, emotionally! You can *see* them…can you not?

There are those in the acts of prostitution and drunkenness!

There are those involved in child molestation, murder, and rape! Thievery! Lust! Envy! Sloth!

I have told you so! Have you not read it in My Word?

!Listen! LISTEN, dear one! **Listen to your LORD**!

The only thing that matters, is the **salvation** of those for whom I shed My Blood!

I have told you before…pray outside your own circle of family, friends, acquaintances! Do you understand what I am saying?

Pray for…

…Your cities and towns!

…Your states and counties!

…Your country, and other countries, as well!

Lift them up to Me, and I will lift them up to the Father!

The more you *praise* Me, the more *blessings* and *glory* you bring to ABBA!

You are placed on this Earth to be an example…a witness…with your own life…so that those who watch you, may see how you live, because **you know Me**!

♥ LOVE UNCONDITIONALLY…AS I LOVE YOU ♥

You can speak of all the Scripture you may remember…all the Scripture that you know! However, it will not bring one soul to salvation *without witnessing*…seeing My people *living those words* every day…and through every circumstance!

* Our work is not yet done!
* I am still raising up Prophets and Messengers!

Until the day I take you Home…your Blessed Assignments are to continue!

For the perishable must clothe itself with the imperishable, and the mortal with immortality. When the perishable has been clothed with the imperishable, and the mortal with immortality, then the saying that is written will come true: "Death has been swallowed up in victory."

"Where, O death, is your victory?

"Where, O death, is your sting?"

1 CORINTHIANS 15:53-58

Remember when I told you to *whisper My Name?* Whisper it often, My child!

- ♥ Praise Me! PRAISE ME, My dear one!
- ♥ GLORIFY the FATHER!
- ♥ ADORE the SAVIOR!
- ♥ Give THANKSGIVING to the HOLY SPIRIT!

I can do everything through him who gives me strength. PHILIPPIANS 4:13

The world has *nothing* for you, My cherished one! You do not belong here! You must pass through this life, on your way to your Eternal Home!

- ♥ Come! Sit beside Me!

…Here! Take a sip of My Living Water!

…Take My hand! Do you feel My strength?

- ♥ Come! I will watch over you each night…and will awaken you each morning!
- ♥ Come! I will fill you with My *peace* that surpasses human understanding!

✝ I LOVE YOU!
✝ YOU ARE MY BELOVED!
✝ THERE IS NO MEASURE TO MY LOVE FOR YOU!

I Am LORD of lords…KING of kings!
  Jesus, the Christ

Precious Sweet-one:

What I tell you in the dark, speak in the daylight;
what is whispered in your ear, proclaim from the roofs.
Do not be afraid of those who kill the body but cannot kill the soul. Rather,
be afraid of the One who can destroy both soul and body in hell.
MATTHEW 10:27-28

! HOW TO SHOW MY MERCY !

"Woe to you, teachers of the law and Pharisees, you hypocrites! You give a tenth of your spices—mint, dill and cummin. But you have neglected the more important matters of the law—justice, mercy and faithfulness. You should have practiced the latter, without neglecting the former. You blind guides! You strain out a gnat but swallow a camel.
MATTHEW 23:23-24

If you had known what these words mean, 'I desire mercy, not sacrifice,' you would not have condemned the innocent. For the Son of Man is Lord of the Sabbath.
MATTHEW 12:7-8

For I desire mercy, not sacrifice, and acknowledgement of God rather than burnt offerings.
HOSEA 6:6

O' My Faithful and Merciful Disciple,

You have wondered as to *when, how* and *to whom* you should *show mercy?*

You have wondered why your LORD *shows mercy* to people *you think* do not deserve it? However, you are only weighing it with man's judgment... not GOD's!

Have you not asked these questions?

Many of Our disciples have not reached the Spiritual Realm of understanding, what I, your LORD, has said in My Word!

When your LORD was on Earth, there were situations in which My first disciples became perplexed, annoyed, or even angry at Me!

The Sons of Thunder, James and John, as well as Peter, would be the first to come to Me and say, "Master, why are you allowing that man to throw a stone at you without using Your power, or even defending yourself...and *telling him Who You are?!*"

I would say again, what I have told them many times: "Oh Peter, dear James, blessed John! There are times we must wait for GOD to present the *perfect opportunity* to address such an action!

There will be a day, when each of us will meet again! I am showing that man GOD's 'MERCY'...not GOD'S 'WRATH'!"

Speak and act as those who are going to be judged by the law that gives freedom, because judgment without mercy will be shown to anyone who has not been merciful. Mercy triumphs over judgment! JAMES 2:12-13

There was a day, as we journeyed to Galilee, when we met a family who lived by the sea! Their 'house' was a homemade tent!

The father, and his two young sons, fished to feed themselves, and to sell some for a meager living!

The mother collected seashells with her three year old daughter! The child was born with one leg shorter than the other! She was also blind in one eye, from a severe storm which caused sand to hit her face!

The mother and daughter spent many hours collecting the best shells they could find! Afterwards, they would string the shells together, to sell on the streets of Galilee!

The earnings they made from selling the fish and necklaces of shells, barely kept them alive!

One day, some rich merchants came upon their tent! Far off they saw the girl hobbling along on the sand! The rest of the family was away; all working for the day's needs!

When they reached town, they inquired about the 'tent family by the sea'!

Everyone they asked had kind words to say about them!

The next day, the merchants decided to see for themselves, if all the kindnesses shown by this family were actually true!

They gave some beggars the fine clothing they wore, in exchange for their tattered clothes!

Dressed now as 'beggars', they went again to find the *family by the sea*!

That day, they saw others who had also made their 'homes' of hand-made tents of rags! They, too, fished for their own needs!

They approached the first tent and asked for some leftover food! They were chased away!

The same thing occurred at the second and third tents!

Then they approached the family who worked twice as hard for their needs!

'Please', the one merchant begged! 'Do you have any food to spare?'

The daughter walked over to the merchant, and taking him by the hand, led him to her father!'

'Abba', she said, 'these men are very hungry! I know why I love you, but these men do not! Will you show them *why?*'

The father smiled, and gently touched her cheek!

'Come', he said to the merchants, 'My wife has just prepared our evening meal! Come and sup with us! We do not have an abundance of food, but whatever we have, we will share with you!'

'Come! Welcome to our home!'

After their prayer, all ate fresh fish, and shared sweet drinks; they even ate fruits and bread!

Their laughter, from the stories they shared, was heard far down the seashore!

The next morning, the merchants returned to their rented rooms! They went into the city, and searched for the best tentmaker!

The next day, the family went about their business, as usual!

When they returned in the mid-afternoon, they could not find their tent!

On the same spot, sat a most elegant tent! People were surrounding it—in awe!

As the family approached, a few of the people ran to them, to tell them what had happened to their *tent of rags*!

They were stunned!

At the entrance stood a man, who explained that two rich merchants wanted to thank them for their generosity!

"They came to my place of business, and were excited to purchase the finest tent I had!"

"They had me help them fill baskets, which are on the table, with all kinds of delicious foods!"

"They also paid me, and others, to be sure you do not go one more day without fresh food! And, to have your family choose whatever clothing you need!"

"Then, I am so happy to tell you, that your little girl is to have the finest medical care! I know a man who has the power to heal! He has been asked to stop here on His way to Jerusalem!"

"Blessings to all of you!"

After this they left!

The family was in such awe, they entered their new home, with PRAISE and GLORY to the Father!

- ♥ After they feasted, they all agreed to set aside a room in the tent! This was for anyone passing through their village, and needed food and lodging, but did not have enough money to pay…and would have to sleep on the ground in the cold of night!
- ♥ They asked each visitor to PRAISE GOD with them!

♥ They told of how their little girl had been healed!

However, they did not say Who healed her, because I asked them not to tell anyone!

Each time, they began their prayers by saying:

But in your great mercy you did not put an end to them or abandon them, for you are a gracious and merciful God. NEHEMIAH 9:31

Now, dearest disciple, tell Me how one *act of mercy* grew and multiplied, as the grains of sand by the sea!

Will you show *mercy* to those I bring to *you?* Family, friends, strangers, and even enemies?

Will you?

Show LOVE and MERCY, as does your LORD,
WHO LOVES YOU BEYOND THE MEASURE
YOU DECIDE ON FOR OTHERS!

I Am He Who Loves Mercy!
The Most Merciful One,
Your KING of kings,
   Jesus, the LORD

Precious Sweet-one:

He has showed you, O man, what is good.
And what does the LORD require of you?
To act justly and to love mercy
and to walk humbly with your God.
MICAH 6:8

! THE STAIRWAY TO HEAVEN... IS NOT STEEP!

"Let not your heart be troubled;
you believe in God, believe also in Me.
"In My Father's house are many mansions; if it were not so,
I would have told you. I go to prepare a place for you.
"And if I go and prepare a place for you, I will come again
and receive you to Myself; that where I am,
there you may be also.
"And where I go you know, and the way you know."
Thomas said to Him, "Lord, we do not know where You
are going, and how can we know the way?"
Jesus said to him, "I am the way, the truth, and the life.
No one comes to the Father except through Me.
JOHN 14:1-6 NKJV

O' My Beloved Disciple,

Our true friends and believers are loved and treasured, more than you could ever imagine!

This is also beyond the most intelligent among you!

However, an *innocent* child and an adult man or woman, with the mind of a child, *accepts*...and *understands*...pure and unconditional LOVE!

- ♥ This LOVE, is of a Divine Nature!
- ♥ This LOVE, comes only from ELOHIM!
- ♥ This LOVE, is impossible to achieve...without infilling from the HOLY SPIRIT!
- ♥ This LOVE, paves the way to HEAVEN for an eternity with the FATHER!
- ♥ This LOVE, was exemplified on the CROSS by JESUS, the CHRIST!

Do you, dear heart, desire to climb My stairway, in order to light the way for others...one *glorious* and *pain-filled step* at a time?

Think on this...

"Let your light so shine before men, that they may see your good works and glorify your Father in heaven. MATTHEW 5:16 NKJV

The way of the just is uprightness;

O Most Upright.

You weigh the path of the just. ISAIAH 26:7 NKJV

Listen carefully, O precious disciple! Each step of the HOLY STAIRCASE...is guarded by two Angels!

One has been assigned for each step!

There are many things you must understand, before you climb each step!

† A disciple of the Messiah—JESUS of Nazareth—Son of Man—only begotten Son of GOD—must learn how to *die to self* while in this life!

† A disciple of the Living GOD...must *grow spiritually* in a myriad of ways...in order to climb each step in the Heavenly Realms!

† A disciple...who *desires* to be faithful and true... available for every Divine Assignment...must keep the mind and heart always on the *goals* of JEHOVAH-tsidkenu—your righteousness!

This *righteousness* must be sought through JEHOVAH-jireh—your Provider and your Vision!

Pray, dearest disciple, in the power of the Holy Spirit...to achieve the *spiritual* and *mental* knowledge, discernment, and understanding...for daily focus and strength!

My heavenly steps become *steeper* due to disobedience and following after worldly wants and desires!

When a disciple turns from the ways of the Savior...the steps become almost impossible to climb!

Have you **understood**?

Have you **listened**?

Have you **believed**?

Am I **not** the LORD of lords?

Am I **not** the KING of kings?

Am I **not** the REDEEMER of all?

Am I **not ELOHIM**, Creator GOD?

A man's heart plans his way,
But the LORD directs his steps. PROVERBS 16:9 NKJV

Therefore, you O man, and you, O woman, must learn how to help others find the narrow pathway...leading to the steps to Heaven's Gate!

Those who are physically disabled...being deaf or blind...or lacking much intellectual understanding...*will climb My holy stairway*...much easier than those who are not!

Do not be dismayed, dear disciple! For those I speak of have *sought* and *found* much more *spiritual health* and *abilities* than those who have not!

Have you sought spiritual wisdom, dearest one?

Is this spiritual wisdom guiding your heart and soul, mind and spirit?

All who have *said* they are disciples, or followers of the CHRIST... are not!

These will find My Holy Stairway very steep, indeed!

These lack the *spiritual discipline* which is necessary to find the *narrow way* to even the first step!

This saddens EL GIBBOR—GOD Almighty—as He looks and sees clearly from His Throne Room!

"Enter by the narrow gate; for wide is the gate and broad is the way that leads to destruction, and there are many who go in by it. "Because narrow is the gate and difficult is the way which leads to life, and there are few who find it. MATTHEW 7:13-14 NKJV

Open your eyes, O man!

Open your eyes, O woman!

See your fellow man stumbling on the way!

See the Enemy's vile cohorts warring against the mighty Angel Army... to win the souls of My creation!

Do NOT turn your eyes to the right...nor to the left...neither look behind you...lest you stumble and fall!

The steps to My Holy Stairway become steeper to climb!

> *Teach me your way, O LORD,*
> *And lead me in a smooth path, because of my enemies.*
> *Do not deliver me to the will of my adversaries;*
> *For false witnesses have risen against me,*
> *And such as breathe out violence.*
> PSALM 27:11-12 NKJV

Listen to the LORD GOD Almighty, dearest disciple!

Recognize a *false witness* immediately...by seeking *discernment* and *insight* from the HOLY SPIRIT!

My true friends and followers **must** stay *spiritually acute*...especially in these last days!

Hear Me, dearest heart, you **must** learn to pray against the *blindness* of your family and friends...who are covered by the *veils* of the Enemy!

Satan and his cohorts do *everything* and *anything* to prevent men, women, and even children, from gaining spiritual strength to climb the Blessed Stairway into the heavenly realms!

My Warrior Angels are always in the battle to protect and guide our believers from the Enemy and his cohorts!

Remember how Our prophets, disciples, and apostles have fought through a myriad of spiritual, mental, emotional, physical, and financial battles to keep themselves from succumbing to the wiles of Satan and his evil followers!

♥ Be aware…always, cherished disciple!
♥ Be aware…alert in the spirit, dear one!
♥ Be aware…the world is in evil turmoil, beloved!

However, as the time for My return is much sooner than most people believe…the HOLY SPIRIT is hovering over all…in answer to your Prayers of Intercession…to **lift off the veils of spiritual ignorance** and of:

…spiritual stubbornness!

…spiritual complacency!

…spiritual hard-heartedness!

…spiritual disobedience!

…spiritual worldliness!

…spiritual sins of all kinds, which sadden the LORD GOD Almighty!

…spiritual blindness which places a wall before My Holy Stairway!

Therefore, precious disciple, the prayers must continue ever more fervently, and with your spiritual language, and with fasting!

As you are able to see each step to climb…one of My Mighty Angels will be with you…to be sure you do not *fall back!*

When you reach the top step…it will be My Hand you will see… outstretched to take hold of your hand and lead you to the mansion I have prepared for you, alone, My blessed disciple!

As you continue your earthly journey…make David's declaration of faith, your own!

Wait on the LORD;
Be of good courage,
And He shall strengthen your heart;
Wait, I say, on the LORD!
PSALM 27:14 NKJV

Come…keep your eyes on your REDEEMER!
Come…stay filled with the JOY of the LORD!
Come…never doubt that the SAVIOR…
LOVES YOU BEYOND MEASURE!

Your KING,
Jesus

! ARE YOU DOUBTING ME? !

If any of you lacks wisdom, he should ask God, who gives generously to all without finding fault, and it will be given to him. But when he asks, he must believe and not doubt, because he who doubts is like a wave of the sea, blown and tossed by the wind. That man should not think he will receive anything from the Lord; he is a double-minded man, unstable in all he does.
JAMES 1:5-8

O' My Dearest Friend,

The Father, Mighty God, El Gibbor, values highly, My friendship with you!

What a blessing it must be to you…to not only be one of My chosen disciples…but, also, one of My closest and faithful friends!

However, there is something even more valuable to your LORD, which blesses Him, and brings glory to our ABBA!

I have mentioned it many times, when I was with the apostles and disciples and have spoken of it, to your heart, often!

O My cherished friend! Each day…each moment of your life…you strive to be faithful and obedient, to fight temptation, to listen for My voice, to be in prayer!

In order to accomplish all of these, there is only one thing that you need for all of them…TO BELIEVE!

To truly…without even an iota of doubt…*BELIEVE!*

- ♥ Believe in your LORD…when you ask for more *strength* to be faithful!
- ♥ Believe in your LORD…when you ask for more *spiritual insight* to be obedient!
- ♥ Believe in your LORD…when you ask for more *protection* to fight off temptations from the Enemy!
- ♥ Believe in your LORD…when you ask for more *quiet times* to hear My voice…to listen…more intently!
- ♥ Believe in your LORD…when you are *Interceding in Prayer* through the power of the HOLY SPIRIT, Who lifts each one before the Father in the Throne Room!

Each prayer, through yielded hearts, is answered by the Father, *according to His perfect will*, and in His *perfect timing!*

While you wait…have no doubts!

Realize, dear one, your LORD will *not abandon* you to become frustrated…where you would lose all hope…then sink into pits of despair and desperation!

Your Friend…Who is Loving, Faithful, and Trustworthy…is always at your side to pick you up when you fall!

♥ This *unconditional love*…is straight from *My Heart*!

Do you doubt this?

When you worship your LORD and KING…what is it you think about?

* How you will worship Me?
* Why you will worship Me?
* When you will worship Me?
* With what you will worship Me?

This is almost the same conversation I had with My prophet, Micah!

With what shall I come before the LORD and bow down before the exalted God? Shall I come before him with burnt offerings, with calves a year old? MICAH 6:6

Sacrifices like these are no longer necessary…nor desired, from Almighty GOD!

Have you not heard? I, your LORD of lords and KING of kings…paid the ultimate price of any sacrifice!

† I died!
† I was entombed!
† I rose from the dead!
† I ascended into Heaven!
† I sit at the right hand of the Father…ELOHIM…the Creator!
† **AND…I WILL RETURN FOR YOU!**

Do you believe these Truths, which I reveal to you?

Listen, dear friend, there can be *no shred of doubt* between us!

Do you remember reading in My Word, about the fig tree?

It was the day after My triumphal entry into Jerusalem!

I was quite weary, My years on Earth, were coming to an end!

I kept seeing the faces in front of Me, of all those who called out, 'HOSANNA TO THE SON OF DAVID'! Knowing, that some of those same faces would be crying out, 'CRUCIFY HIM'…just a few days later!

Then, My righteous anger—when I entered the temple area! I was not angry in the human sense! I was angry, that My Beloved Elohim had had to watch the exchange of the selling of doves and unblemished lambs; including the 'money changers'…all taking advantage of those who were coming to worship in My Father's House!

Early the next morning, we were hungry, as we were on our way back into the city…I saw a fig tree with nothing but leaves!

The apostles and disciples were in amazement when I said to the tree: *"May you never bear fruit again."*

Immediately the tree withered!

They did not know whether to laugh or cry, or walk away!

As I heard them asking, 'How did the fig tree wither so quickly'?

Jesus replied, "I tell you the truth, if you have faith and do not doubt, not only can you do what was done to the fig tree, but also you can say to this mountain, 'Go, throw yourself into the sea,' and it will be done. If you believe, you will receive whatever you ask for in prayer." MATTHEW 21:21-22

It is the same with your worship of Me!

You must *believe…have no doubts…*of Who I Truly Am!

Then, your worship will bring Glory to the Father, Who sees all!

Yet a time is coming and has now come when the true worshipers will worship the Father in spirit and truth, for they are the kind of worshipers the Father seeks. God is spirit, and his worshipers must worship in spirit and in truth." JOHN 4:23-24

Have no doubts, about anything which I have spoken to you in these messages!

As hearts are being readied for the events, which were foretold long ago…and will continue to unfold as have been prophesied!

My chosen must learn how to encourage each other, through these last days!

Your love for one another, will testify loudly to the world, that you are My true *followers,* My *friends!*

♥ Come, dear friend! Continue to yearn to return to your Heavenly Home, as you rest in My arms!

♥ Come, dear faithful and obedient one, close your eyes! Imagine the day you will be drinking and eating at the Banquet Table with your Adonai!

I, YOUR SAVIOR, LOVE YOU BEYOND
THE MEASURE OF HOLINESS!

Yesua ha'Machiach

Precious Sweet-one:

Jesus wept.
JOHN 11:35
I wept, beloved disciples, because of the people's UNBELIEF!

! I OFFER YOU HOPE
AND A FUTURE !

For I know the plans I have for you," declares the LORD, "plans to prosper you and not to harm you, plans to give you hope and a future.
JEREMIAH 29:11

O' My Dear and Chosen Child,
- ♥ Have I not told you how much I love you?
- ♥ Have I not told you the plans I have for you?

I offer you a hope and a future!

However, I hear you say, "LORD, at this stage of my life, what kind of *future* could you possibly have for *me?*"

O My dear child! Do you not remember when you became Born Again? Yes, you are still human in this world…on Earth! But your spirit, and your soul…have stepped over the Threshold into My Eternal Realm!

You *yearn* for Home…do you not?

You *yearn* to be with your LORD and SAVIOR… together with ABBA…and the HOLY SPIRIT! Do you not?

If you belonged to the world, it would love you as its own. As it is, you do not belong to the world, but I have chosen you out of the world. That is why the world hates you. JOHN 15:19

I tell you the truth…ABBA and your LORD desire for you…and all Our chosen…to be Home again with Us!

"Again LORD! When have I ever been there?"

Have you not read My Word?

O dear one! I knew you *before* you were born!

I knew you *before* the worlds were made! This is a mystery you will understand when you reach Home!

Because of sin, My chosen had to take this road through Earth to return to Me! And I had to come to Earth and die on the Cross…in order that My Blood would atone for the sin of mankind!

For the one whom God has sent speaks the words of God, for God gives the Spirit without limit. The Father loves the Son and has placed everything in his hands. Whoever believes in the Son has eternal life, but whoever rejects the Son will not see life, for God's wrath remains on him." JOHN 3:34-36

When I left Glory and walked on Earth, I remembered My Home in Heaven, and yearned to return to the Father!

My heart was sorrowful when I had to leave My apostles and disciples! But I knew, that they would be coming to Me, one day soon!

Because of the original sin of Adam and Eve...man must suffer *mortality*!

Only those who BELIEVE in the SON OF GOD's sacrifice...will put on *immortality* and live eternally with GOD, His Saints, and His Angels!

Do not *fret* over those, whom you love, who have not yet accepted Me!

Because of your *faithfulness*, your *obedience*, and because of your *love* for Me...because of your desire to see your loved ones saved, as well as friends, strangers and even enemies...you will be surprised as to whom you will meet in the Heavenly dimensions!

Fret not, My child!

The Father, our ABBA, is pleased with your Sacrifices of Praise for all you endure!

♥ Am I not your friend?

♥ Am I not your *best* friend?

♥ Am I not your *All-in-All*?

For my Father's will is that everyone who looks to the Son and believes in him shall have eternal life, and I will raise him up at the last day." JOHN 6:40

Then, and only then, will you be able to *completely separate* yourself from the attachments of those in the world! Yes...even your loved ones!

Learn from Me, to *detach* yourself from the world!

The world, My child, includes all you have; especially, what you desire... spiritually, emotionally, physically, and financially!

Even your assignments from Me, should not matter as much as your *relationship* with Me...your LORD of lords...your KING of kings!

I am your Adonai, your Master, not as master to slave!

As your Adonai, I Am your Teacher!

You are no longer My servant...you are My *friend*!

As My friend, I desire to teach you 'heavenly secrets'...for you to see into the 'heavenly dimensions'!

The HOLY SPIRIT will give you *spiritual insight* to discern **what** and **who** are from the Enemy—Satan; and clearly **see** all which comes from your LORD—JESUS, the Messiah!

♥ Am I not your Treasure...as you are Mine?

...There is nothing you need!

...There is nothing you should want!

...There is nothing you should desire...outside of your relationship with Me!

♥ This is the *witness* I require of you! It is not the work that you *think* you are doing for Me, that is important!

It is how you *react* in the face of adversity!

That is your *witness*! That is what you are to *strive to learn* from Me!

When you ask for *strength* from the Holy Spirit, the *strength* is to know *when to speak* and *when not to speak*…in the presence of those who do not know Me, and who reject or laugh at you!

I tell you the truth, anyone who has faith in me will do what I have been doing. He will do even greater things than these, because I am going to the Father. And I will do whatever you ask in my name, so that the Son may bring glory to the Father. You may ask me for anything in my name, and I will do it. JOHN 14:12-14

♥ Keep your eyes on Me!

♥ Do not look to the *right* nor to the *left*!

♥ Do not look *behind* you! **LOOK TO ME!**

The past is past…GONE!

† Your future awaits you with your LORD, your Savior, your Christ!

Just as *I* ascended into Heaven…*you* will ascend, as well!

Peace I leave with you; my peace I give you. I do not give to you as the world gives. Do not let your hearts be troubled and do not be afraid. JOHN 14:27

Come! Sit with Me!

Take the Cup of My Living Water and drink thirstily! Drink, dearest one!

Come! Take My hand! Let us walk in the moonlight!

Picture yourself walking in the sand with your LORD, and the waves gently lapping our feet with ribbons of moonlight on the water…glistening…sparkling…like jewels from Heaven!

Remember…My Love For You Has No End…

It Is Beyond Measure!

Your Friend and Lover,
Yeshua

! WHO AM I...TO YOU? !

Jesus and his disciples went on to the villages around
Caesarea Philippi. On the way he asked them,
"Who do people say I am?"
They replied, "Some say John the Baptist;
others say Elijah; and still others, one of the prophets."
"But what about you?" he asked. "Who do you say I am?"
Peter answered, "You are the Christ."
Jesus warned them not to tell anyone about him.
MARK 8:27-30

O' My Dearest Friend, My Faithful Disciple,

Our ABBA sends His love to you...through the power of the Holy Spirit!

As you read or hear these words...you should feel Our LOVE fill you more and more!

♥ Our LOVE is akin to the Holy Spring of Living Water!

♥ Our LOVE is akin to the in-filling of Blessed Joy!

♥ Our LOVE is akin to the Perfect Peace that surpasses human understanding!

All of these are given to you freely...so that you, dear one, will overflow Love, Joy and Peace...to all whom you know and meet!

Now, I ask you, "Who am I to *you?*"

You know, do you not, why I told My apostles and disciples...who recognized Who I was...not to reveal this to anyone?

It would have been impossible for Me to easily complete My mission on Earth!

† There were some who would try to put Me to death, before the appointed time!

† There were those who would have taken Me by force...to make Me a *human king*!

† There were those who would have mobbed Me...to merely touch Me to heal every single person...men, women, and children!

They would have treated your LORD as a 'magician'!

Am I a *human king* to you? Perhaps you have some family members, or friends, who view Me as such!

Am I a 'magic' type of god? One whom you ask to do a 'trick' of healing... or shower you with 'riches'?

Are there members among you, who feel this way about Me?

Perhaps you, or others you know, follow the preaching of Pastors who tell you, 'You have the power to call down God into your situation, and He will do whatever you need...or *give* you whatever you want!?'

It is all about 'prosperity religion'!

Is this Who or what I am to *you*, dear one?

Have you read Hannah's prayer? Hannah was one of two wives married to Elkanah! His other wife, Peninnah, had given him many children!

But, Hannah, having none, had to endure day after day, constant belittling from Peninnah! So much so, that Hannah would weep until she could not eat!

She came to the house of the LORD!

In bitterness of soul Hannah wept much and prayed to the LORD! And she made a vow, saying,

"O LORD Almighty, if you will only look upon your servant's misery and remember me and do not forget your servant but give her a son, then I will give him to the LORD for all the days of his life, and no razor will ever be used on his head." 1 SAMUEL 1:10-11

I gave her a son! And, good to her word...she gave that son back to Me! She named him *Samuel*...meaning, *"Because I asked the LORD for him."*

She kept the vow to the LORD! After weaning him, she took him to the temple!

Can you imagine the *selfless attitude* of Hannah?

* She *knew* Who I was!
* She *knew* I was the I AM...Who kept His promises! Therefore, Hannah kept hers!

"There is no one holy like the LORD; there is no one besides you; there is no Rock like our God. 1 SAMUEL 2:2

Those days were quite different than today! Are they not?

What would a modern-day 'Hannah' have done?

There are many women, who are barren, and pray to give birth, to even one child!

* Some have their prayers answered with a gentle, 'No, my child, your LORD knows what is best for your life'!
* Some have their prayers answered with a gentle, 'You must wait, My child, it is not time for you, as yet: Your LORD knows what is best for you'!

  * Some have their prayers answered with a gentle, 'Yes, My child, your LORD knows what is best for you'!

Would any woman, reading these words, have given up her child? After waiting a long time to give birth to one? Would you?

If the reader or hearer of these words is a man…and the husband of a woman who is praying for a child…what would you have done?

Who is your LORD…to *you?*

Are you a man after My own heart, as David was?

Do you remember reading the parable of the blind man recorded by John?

The apostles wanted to know, if there was sin in the blind man, or if his parents had sinned…is this why he was born blind?

Could Hannah's parents have sinned…and closed her womb?

If you are ill, or suffer with constant pain…is this due to *your sin*…or that of your *parents?*

What **kind** of God are you serving?

Who am I to **you?**

"Neither this man nor his parents sinned," said Jesus, "but this happened so that the work of God might be displayed in his life. As long as it is day, we must do the work of him who sent me. Night is coming, when no one can work. While I am in the world, I am the light of the world." JOHN 9:3-5

  ✦ Do others see Me…in you?
  ✦ Do others hear Me…from you?
  ✦ Do others love Me…through you?
  ✦ Do others obey Me…because of you?

WHO am I to *others?*

…a GOD of JOY?

…a GOD of PEACE?

…a GOD of COMFORT?

…a GOD of PROMISES?

…a GOD of ETERNAL LIFE?

…a GOD of FAITHFULNESS?

Remember, My dear disciple…I Am the LORD of lords and the KING of kings…your LORD…your KING…Who Loves You Unconditionally…Beyond Measure!

With All My Heart,
The Christ,
 Jesus

Precious Sweet-one:

On the last and greatest day of the Feast, Jesus stood and said in a loud voice, "If anyone is thirsty, let him come to me and drink. Whoever believes in me, as the Scripture has said, streams of living water will flow from within him."
JOHN 7:37-38

! IT IS THAT SIMPLE !

*For this reason I kneel before the Father, from whom his whole family
in heaven and on earth derives its name. I pray that out of his glorious
riches he may strengthen you with power through his Spirit in your inner
being, so that Christ may dwell in your hearts through faith. And I pray
that you, being rooted and established in love, may have power, together
with all the saints, to grasp how wide and long and high and deep is the
love of Christ, and to know this love that surpasses knowledge—that you
may be filled to the measure of all the fullness of God. Now to him who
is able to do immeasurably more than all we ask or imagine, according
to his power that is at work within us, to him be glory in the church and
in Christ Jesus throughout all generations, for ever and ever! Amen.*
EPHESIANS 3:14-21

O' My Blessed Brothers and Sisters,

Our ABBA has asked for each of you to be anointed with His special touch!

Just as I, your LORD, assembled the apostles and disciples, many times as we journeyed…I must also gather you to Myself!

I know you have many questions…of Heaven…of Hell…of death and the process of dying…of your own judgment…and most essentially…of your own existence and the role you are to play on the *eternal stage of life!*

You are not as 'little children' who have to be taught how to crawl! You have *crawled*; you learned to *walk*; now, you need to learn how to *run*!

Be imitators of God, therefore, as dearly loved children and live a life of love, just as Christ loved us and gave himself up for us as a fragrant offering and sacrifice to God. EPHESIANS 5:1-2

Why have you accepted Me, JESUS, as your Christ—the Messiah?

…Remember how you *first heard* about Me?

…Did your *heart* and *spirit* hear Me *knocking*?

…Was someone you know, constantly talking about how they *received Salvation?*

…Did someone, near and dear to you, suddenly change …from being somewhat *hard hearted*…to being quite *loving and caring?*

…Were they at peace, after suffering from a *traumatic experience?*

…Was their life filled with sadness…and now…*in spite of circumstances*… they now exhibit Joy?

It is not difficult to understand! It is quite simple!

Dear one…they met the Savior!
They were filled with the Holy Spirit!

† Have you not read, or heard the accounts, written by those who were *witnesses* of My Life…Death…and Resurrection?

† After My Ascension into Heaven…what a *glorious* day that was for Me…I finally returned to My Home in Heaven!

† However, because of My Ascension to Heaven, I was able to send the HOLY SPIRIT to fill the hearts of men, women, and children…until the day of My return…to take all True Believers of the CHRIST… to be where I AM!

The apostles and disciples waited anxiously in the upper room where they were staying! They numbered one hundred and twenty!

During this time, they were in constant prayer…along with the women and Mary, My earthly mother, and my brothers and sisters!

When the day of Pentecost came, they were all together in one place. Suddenly a sound like the blowing of a violent wind came from heaven and filled the whole house where they were sitting. They saw what seemed to be tongues of fire that separated and came to rest on each of them. All of them were filled with the Holy Spirit and began to speak in other tongues as the Spirit enabled them. ACTS 2:1-4

† Their lives changed *radically* and *dramatically!*

† No mystery to this…is there?

† You know now…do you not?

The *Holy Spirit* filled your *heart, mind, spirit* and *soul*…you have never been the same since…have you, cherished soul!?

Now, dearest and most precious friend, you desire for others…not only loved ones…but every one whose path crosses yours…to experience the *absolute* JOY of becoming Born-Again!

It is a *spiritual frustration* to you, cherished disciple, why so many *refuse* a relationship with the LORD of lords…is it not?

You desire to experience what happened to Peter, and the others, on that first Pentecost…do you not?

Peter went out on the balcony and spoke:

"Therefore let all Israel be assured of this: God has made this Jesus, whom you crucified, both Lord and Christ." When the people heard this, they were cut to the heart and said to Peter and the other apostles, "Brothers, what shall we do?" ACTS 2:36-37

It was simple!

Peter was so excited…he told them that they had to **repent** and be **baptized**, in the name of JESUS Christ, for the forgiveness of their sins!

Then...they would receive the HOLY SPIRIT!

Simple! Accept the Christ as their personal Savior and LORD...and they would be BORN-AGAIN...their sins forgiven...and be given Eternal Life with the GOD of their fathers!

O dearly treasured one, pray for Holy boldness, to *tell those whose hearts are ready...*that My promises are for you, your children, and everyone to the last generation...whom the LORD GOD will call!

- ♥ Accepting JESUS as your personal LORD...is simple!
- ♥ Learning about Who I AM, and how to know Me...is written in the Holy Scriptures!
- ♥ Call out My Name!
- ♥ Speak to Me!
- ♥ You will hear Me answer...in and through every recess of your heart...mind...and spirit!
- ♥ Call out to Me!
- ♥ Listen intently for My 'whispers'! Allow your LORD to teach *you*... as I taught the first apostles and disciples!
- ♥ Stand in My Shadow...for protection against the Enemy!
- ♥ My Love for you transcends Time...Space...Heavenly Dimensions!

What of you?

Will you lean on Me?

Will you learn to lean your cross on Me?

Because of My Crucifixion, Death, and Resurrection, no one's 'cross' will be unbearable!

"Come to me, all you who are weary and burdened, and I will give you rest. Take my yoke upon you and learn from me, for I am gentle and humble in heart, and you will find rest for your souls. For my yoke is easy and my burden is light."
MATTHEW 11:28-30

The KING of kings...Loves You Beyond Measure!

Your ADONAI,
Jesus, the Messiah

Precious Sweet-one:

Dear friends, I urge you, as aliens and strangers in the world, to abstain from sinful desires, which war against your soul. Live such good lives among the pagans that, though they accuse you of doing wrong, they may see your good deeds and glorify God on the day he visits us.
1 PETER 2:11-12

! DO YOU SEE ME? WHERE AM I?

My soul finds rest in God alone;
my salvation comes from him.
PSALM 62:1

I seek you with all my heart;
do not let me stray from your commands.
I have hidden your word in my heart
that I might not sin against you.
Praise be to you, O LORD;
teach me your decrees.
PSALM 119:10-12

Seek the LORD while he may be found;
call on him while he is near.
ISAIAH 55:6

"I revealed myself to those who did not ask for me;
I was found by those who did not seek me.
To a nation that did not call on my name,
I said, 'Here am I, here am I.'
ISAIAH 65:1

O' My Dear and Faithful Friends,

When you first heard of JESUS of Nazareth…Who was *crucified* for you…and broke the hold of Death by Rising from the dead…you were amazed that you had no, or little, knowledge of the 'Spiritual World'! Were you not?

Due to the Intercessory Prayers of others…each of you became a BORN-AGAIN disciple…of the LORD of lords!

Now you *intercede in prayer* for others to see the **TRUTH** and be set **Free!**

When people wonder about your Faith in Christ…you now have *spiritual eyes* to see how much *deception* the Enemy has placed on them!

After My 'resurrection', many *tried* to deceive My disciples!

The guards at My tomb were paid to *lie*…that My disciples came in the middle of the night, and took My Body away!

♥ Do you, precious disciple, **truly believe** that your SAVIOR **LIVES?**

♥ Do you, cherished friend, **actually believe** that many men, women, and even children, *would die for a myth?*

♥ Do you, chosen disciple, **have proof** that you have been filled by the HOLY SPIRIT…as My very first followers were…and became *BORN-AGAIN?*

♥ Do you, believing disciple, expect **to be Risen from the dead**…*and forever be with your LORD in Paradise?*

♥ Do you, faithful disciple, **believe from your heart** that GOD did as He promised…and sent His Only Begotten Son to be the Final Blood Sacrifice…the **True Lamb of GOD?**

Where do you *see* Me in your world?

How do you *look* for Me, in your particular life-style?

What do you *hear* about Me, the GOD of your *fathers?*

When do you *see* a manifestation of your LORD GOD?

…in healings?

…in restorations?

…in forgiveness?

…in mercy?

…in grace?

…in atonements?

* Am I not in the *first smile* of a newborn babe?

* Am I not in the *light* of a loved one's eyes?

* Am I not in the *embrace* of a brother or sister in the LORD?

Cherished disciple! Where do **you** *see Me?*

In the *eyes* of a beggar?

On the *face* of a beloved spouse?

What exactly are **you** looking for…in order to see the Face of GOD?

Have you looked into a mirror…and not seen your face…but the CHRIST'S Light in your own eyes?

When you reach the place in your walk with Me…where your *heart, mind, spirit,* and *soul* desire **nothing**, nor **anyone**…other than your KING JESUS…then, My dearest disciple, you will see **Me everywhere** you look!

Every where…

In every one…

In every situation…

Your LORD of lords is with you!

"Ask and it will be given to you; seek and you will find; knock and the door

will be opened to you. For everyone who asks receives; he who seeks finds; and to him who knocks, the door will be opened. MATTHEW 7:7-8

Are you truly opening your *spiritual eyes*...to clearly *see Me?*

♥ I could tell you, each moment when I have been next to you!

♥ I could tell you, every moment when I have been holding your hand—and leading you from danger!

♥ I could tell you, whenever you lent a hand to a stranger; or gave a cup of cool water in My Name...I was there!

The woman at the well—a Samaritan—offered to draw water for Me, as I sat on the stone wall around the well! I had nothing—that she could see—for Me to draw water with! However, she was about to be *blessed*, along with many from her village...they received forgiveness, and were accepted among My followers!

She saw a Prophet...then she was about to meet the Messiah, which she had read about...wanting to understand the One True GOD!

The woman said, "I know that Messiah" (called Christ) *"is coming. When he comes, he will explain everything to us."*

Then Jesus declared, "I who speak to you am he." JOHN 4:25-26

My disciples returned as I was speaking with a *Samaritan woman!*

However, they asked no questions; they were only concerned for Me to eat and rest!

! UNCONDITIONAL LOVE !

That is how you, and, everyone else, will see ME...the LORD of lords!

! UNCONDITIONAL FORGIVENESS !

That is how you, and, everyone else, will find ME...the KING of kings!

However, My dear friend, *hearts* must be made ready by the Power of the HOLY SPIRIT!

And Isaiah boldly says, "I was found by those who did not seek me; I revealed myself to those who did not ask for me." ROMANS 10:20

Yes! The Gentiles, nor the pagans, asked for a Deliverer!

However, I chose Paul as a disciple to the Gentiles!

It was not an easy task by any means! He took his commission—a Divine Assignment—very seriously!

After speaking, at length, to Peter and the other disciples and followers, Paul made a final statement—to make them understand:

..."*The Holy Spirit spoke the truth to your forefathers when he said through Isaiah the prophet:*

" 'Go to this people and say,
"You will be ever hearing but never understanding;
you will be ever seeing but never perceiving."
For this people's heart has become calloused;
they hardly hear with their ears,
and they have closed their eyes.
Otherwise they might see with their eyes,
hear with their ears,
understand with their hearts
and turn, and I would heal them.'

"Therefore I want you to know that God's salvation has been sent to the
Gentiles, and they will listen!'
ACTS 28:25-28

Because of this, you, blessed one, will invite…love…forgive…obey…and
be faithful, to extend all your talents, time, and treasures, for the Kingdom,
and lay up treasures in Heaven…for My sake…and to the GLORY of the
Father—Our ABBA!

♥ Keep looking up!
   ♥ Work as you wait for Me!
YOU…BLESSED FOLLOWER…
ARE LOVED BEYOND MEASURE!

Your Redeemer and LORD,
Jesus, The Messiah

! TURN CHAOS INTO PEACE !

Love and faithfulness meet together;
righteousness and peace kiss each other.
PSALM 85:10

"There is no peace," says the LORD, "for the wicked."
ISAIAH 48:22

Peace I leave with you; my peace I give you. I do not give to you as the
world gives. Do not let your hearts be troubled and do not be afraid.
JOHN 14:27

O' My Dearest Children,

You are so precious to Me! The love I feel for you is more than I can tell
you in human words! Only through the power of the Holy Spirit can you
understand the love I have for you!

There is chaos all over the world! Much of this chaos does not touch you…
but you must remember to pray for those who are living in the world's chaos!

You know, dear ones, that this world's chaos is caused by Satan! The
Enemy…yours and Mine!

I know how much you desire for My presence! Do you not? Do you
desire to come home to Me? Is it because you truly desire to be with Me,
your LORD, the Christ? Or, is it because you want to escape the chaos that
is happening all over the Earth?

I know, dearest, there is chaos in too many homes!

There are homes in which one or more of the adults are entrusted with
Treasures from the Elohim, and they abuse and mistreat those treasures!
My heart cries out to them! Those treasures are children who have no power
and no means to escape the daily nightmares!

+ They should feel safe!
+ They should feel loved! Instead, those who are supposed to love them
  are in a state of drunkenness causing them to abuse and misuse My
  treasured children!
+ They do not meet their needs!

O that these little ones could go and escape that life; but they are too
young…and in fear!

"I have told you these things, so that in me you may have peace. In this

world you will have trouble. But take heart! I have overcome the world."
JOHN 16:33

You know this is the work of the Enemy, do you not? You must pray for them, My faithful disciples! You must pray for them! I need you to use My Gift of Intercessory Prayer!

I speak strongly for the little ones, who are left home alone, to fend for themselves, while their guardians are out, spending their money on a good time...while the little ones are starving! Then, if these little ones cry out for food or basic needs, they are beaten!

...Can you see them?

...Can you see the desperation in their eyes?

They are starving for lack of nourishment for their bodies, their minds, hearts and their spirits...for their very souls!

...Will you walk in My steps? When you follow Me, as you say you are, you will see the inhumanity of people to their own kind! Not even the animals act this way!

My dearest disciples, I need to place you in a 'Dome of Protection', especially if you are living in one of these homes, where those around you want to steal your peace, your joy, and above all, your souls away from Me!

♥ Run to Me...**run to Me!**
♥ Come...**into My arms!**
♥ Feel the thickness of the Dome... which I placed over you! **I am in it with you!**

Do you see Me? You can do all the things you need to do inside this Dome; but I am separating you from those who are deep in the world...the Enemy's playpen!

Wherever you go, whatever you do, My Dome surrounds you! You can keep your peace and your joy!

Pray, pray the words of John, My beloved Apostle, *'Greater is he who is in me, than he that is in the world.'* 1 JOHN 4:4

When chaos, frustration, or any of the ploys of the Enemy come out to assault you, remember, YOU are in MY Dome of Protection...and you can pray within your heart, **'Greater, much greater, is He who is in me than anyone or anything that is in the world!'**

Cry out My Name...'JESUS!' 'JESUS!' 'JESUS!'... and I will be there, within the same breath, answering the Enemy's knock on the door of your heart!

Do not leave the door ajar for the Enemy to sneak in...and destroy!

✝ Plead My Blood!

† Surround yourself with those who love Me!

† Gather to *pray,* to *sing,* to *worship,* to *praise* and *adore* the KING of kings!

You need this, My dearest ones!

You need this as an in-filling of courage, an in-filling of spiritual strength!

The Holy Spirit will empower and protect you!

Do you understand, dearest ones?

Do not fret over those who will not listen! They *think* they do! They say they do, but they are misconstruing what I am telling them!

When I tell you to wait, it does not mean for you to stand still and do nothing!

You must occupy your time diligently until I return!

Time is precious on Earth, and because you are in Eternal Time...does not mean I will not show My wrath to those who waste precious time by doing nothing!

When I have you in the waiting rooms, there are still things you must accomplish! Do you understand what I have said, dear disciples?

Do not, in your own strength, try to change those who are in a vicious, stubborn cycle!

Do not toss your wisdom to those who have excuses and love the words "I can not!" There is no such concept in the Heavenly realms!

...Did I not tell you, you can do *all* things through Me who strengthens you?

...Did I not tell you, *nothing* is impossible for Me?

This is how you must *live!*

This is how you must *believe!*

Nothing is impossible for those of you who believe in Me!

♥ Now come, rest beside Me!

♥ Feel My presence!

♥ Listen for My Voice!

I Love You Beyond Measure!

Do you love Me beyond measure, precious children?

You are Mine!

I treasure you!

I am Jehovah-Nissi...your Victory over all!

Your Beloved Savior,
Jesus

ABOUT THE MESSENGER

Dear Reader,

The LORD, Jesus the Christ, is the true Author of this book!

He is the One Who gave me these 'memos', and inspired me to be one of His 'messengers'...through a lifetime of emotional and physical afflictions, and loss!

I was born and raised in Newark, New Jersey, of Sicilian emigrant parents; who were among the 'boat people' in the 1930's that were processed through Ellis Island. My father's name is etched on the wall, which honors many of the emigrants, who traveled thousands of miles from their homes, across the Atlantic Ocean.

My mama died when I was fourteen—the beginning of my heart's losses. Papa followed, twenty years later.

During these twenty years, I married, and gave birth to three children... two daughters and a son...who is the *middle* child, as am I.

We came to California in 1975, leaving behind the only place I knew!

In 1977, I accepted Jesus Christ as My LORD and Savior!

It was in California that more physical ailments pursued me, and the beginning of numerous surgeries, which threatened to take my life. Then the death of my marriage; more surgeries and more diagnoses.

I remarried in 1990, and together, we have five children and eleven grandchildren.

Of these eleven, two of our beloved, have lived in Heaven, since November 2007.

The first of these books was published only a few months before, our then fifteen year old granddaughter, was taken Home!

A copy, with a personal note from me, her 'Mema', is among her stored possessions.

Our grandson, who was taken to Heaven with his sister, was nine at the time! I can just see him perfecting his Karate skills before the LORD!

Six more loved ones were called Home, as I have continued to listen for His messages!

Among them, a nephew in 2008, a brother-in-law in 2009; and my younger sister in March of 2010; along with two of the other grandparents!

My heart and spirit were torn even more, when my only son was found dead, after 6 days, of heart failure in July 2010!

Only my dear and blessed Savior, sustains me and the members of our family, through these earthly losses!

I have dreamt of being a writer and author from the age of three.

Since July 22, 2003, I have written and documented the LORD's messages to me, and to others!

February 24, 2005, He gave me the first of many 'memos'! Then He spoke to my heart to 'self-publish' these memos, which He has continued to give me!

I pray...throughout this endeavor...that each of you is BLESSED as you read...as I am BLESSED as I write!

I continue to listen for His voice...through the power of the Holy Spirit...in spite of my physical and emotional afflictions, and earthly losses. As I have learned to say: PRAISE THE LORD, ANYWAY!

JESUS LOVES ALL OF US...BEYOND MEASURE!

If you have any comments or questions, please contact me at: THELORDSAID@hotmail.com, as it would be a blessing to hear from you!

Salvatrice

✝

I AM WHO AM, call upon all available scribes to tell My people how much THE LIVING and ETERNAL GOD—Almighty and True—yearns for hearts to be ready and accept My free Gift of Salvation!

✝

! JESUS IS WAITING FOR YOU TO COME TO HIM !

Jesus, I know you are the Son of God
and that you rose from the grave!
Thank you for dying on the Cross in my place!
I ask you now to forgive my sins
and come into my heart!
Thank you for saving me!
Thank you for being my LORD and Savior!
Amen!

WHAT I HEARD FROM THE LORD

_____

_____

_____

_____

_____

_____

_____

_____

_____

_____

_____

_____

_____

_____

_____